FLOYD CLYMER'S MOTORCYCLIST'S LIBRARY

The Book of the

B.S.A. SUNBEAM AND TRIUMPH TIGRESS
MOTOR-SCOOTERS

A PRACTICAL GUIDE TO THE HANDLING
AND MAINTENANCE OF ALL MODELS

BY

JOHN THORPE

First published 1963
Reprinted with minor corrections 1967

ANNOUNCEMENT

By special arrangement with the original publishers of this book, Sir Isaac Pitman & Son, Ltd., of London, England, we have secured the exclusive publishing rights for this book, as well as all others in THE MOTORCYCLIST'S LIBRARY.

Included in THE MOTORCYCLIST'S LIBRARY are complete instruction manuals covering the care and operation of respective motorcycles and engines; valuable data on speed tuning, and thrilling accounts of motorcycle race events. See listing of available titles elsewhere in this edition.

We consider it a privilege to be able to offer so many fine titles to our customers.

FLOYD CLYMER
Publisher of Books Pertaining to Automobiles and Motorcycles
2125 W. PICO ST.   LOS ANGELES 6, CALIF.

INTRODUCTION

Welcome to the world of digital publishing ~ the book you now hold in your hand, while unchanged from the original edition, was printed using the latest state of the art digital technology. The advent of print-on-demand has forever changed the publishing process, never has information been so accessible and it is our hope that this book serves your informational needs for years to come. If this is your first exposure to digital publishing, we hope that you are pleased with the results. Many more titles of interest to the classic automobile and motorcycle enthusiast, collector and restorer are available via our website at www.VelocePress.com. We hope that you find this title as interesting as we do.

NOTE FROM THE PUBLISHER

The information presented is true and complete to the best of our knowledge. All recommendations are made without any guarantees on the part of the author or the publisher, who also disclaim all liability incurred with the use of this information.

TRADEMARKS

We recognize that some words, model names and designations, for example, mentioned herein are the property of the trademark holder. We use them for identification purposes only. This is not an official publication.

INFORMATION ON THE USE OF THIS PUBLICATION

This manual is an invaluable resource for the classic motorcycle enthusiast and a "must have" for owners interested in performing their own maintenance. However, in today's information age we are constantly subject to changes in common practice, new technology, availability of improved materials and increased awareness of chemical toxicity. As such, it is advised that the user consult with an experienced professional prior to undertaking any procedure described herein. While every care has been taken to ensure correctness of information, it is obviously not possible to guarantee complete freedom from errors or omissions or to accept liability arising from such errors or omissions. Therefore, any individual that uses the information contained within, or elects to perform or participate in do-it-yourself repairs or modifications acknowledges that there is a risk factor involved and that the publisher or its associates cannot be held responsible for personal injury or property damage resulting from the use of the information or the outcome of such procedures.

WARNING!

One final word of advice, this publication is intended to be used as a reference guide, and when in doubt the reader should consult with a qualified technician.

For your B.S.A SUNBEAM and TRIUMPH TIGRESS SCOOTERS

Be wise when the time comes to renew your battery. Fit Silver Exide. No longer-lasting motor cycle battery is made or has ever been made!

B.S.A SUNBEAM SCOOTERS

1958—63 B1 and B2	3-EV11
1958—63 B2S and B2 (Police)	2/3-EV11
1964—66 B1	3-EV11
1964—66 B2	2/3 EV11

TRIUMPH TIGRESS SCOOTERS

1958—63 TS1 and TW2	3-EV11
1958—63 TW2/S	2/3-EV11

EXIDE—for the power to be sure!

PREFACE

In 1945 when I first started riding, most of us began with ancient motor-cycles which spent rather more of their time in pieces in the garage than in one piece on the road. These old machines of ours were cheap, simple—and expendable.

Today a smart new motor-scooter is within the reach of most people. Scooters are relatively complicated, good value for money (though not by any means cheap), and very definitely *not* expendable.

Hence the rather carefree approach which I, as a novice, was able to make to maintenance 20-odd years ago no longer applies. To strip a modern motor-scooter requires a variety of tools, considerable mechanical knowledge, and ample time to spend on the job. Most of us these days do not possess all three prerequisites.

Most towns now have at least one dealer who maintains a well-equipped workshop staffed with factory-trained mechanics who can do the major work on a scooter quickly, cheaply and well. There is no point in neglecting these facilities by attempting jobs which are out of one's depth. On the other hand, there is no point, either, in dragging a scooter to the dealer, and leaving it there for a day or so, for some trifling adjustment which one could make equally well, oneself, in an hour or less. This is really a question of keeping a sense of proportion.

For this reason I have deliberately restricted the contents of this book to the more elementary work which the private owner can carry out, and some of the chapters are devoted to related subjects, such as the basic working principles and methods of fault tracing, without knowledge of which no work at all can be done.

I have also included a chapter on handling scooters. The way in which a machine is driven, especially during the first few thousand miles, has a considerable bearing upon its reliability, performance, and ultimate "life." A badly-handled machine is apt to be an unreliable machine, even if it is otherwise well maintained.

Also included in the book is a short chapter on the tool kit. It is essential to have the right tools for the job before attempting maintenance of any sort, and it would be most unrealistic to expect the manufacturer—who already has a tough struggle to keep his costs down—to include with each scooter a kit comprehensive enough to enable every single mechanical job to be carried out. Understandably, he includes a kit which is adequate for roadside emergencies and for simple jobs, and leaves the rest to the purchaser.

In the preparation of this book, I have been admirably aided by the B.S.A/Triumph Scooter Division, who provided every scrap of information which I requested; checked the more specialized chapters; and provided a wealth of illustrations.

JOHN THORPE

CONTENTS

CHAP.		PAGE
	Preface	
I.	THE B.S.A./TRIUMPH RANGE	1
II.	BASIC PRINCIPLES	5
III.	HANDLING SCOOTERS	19
IV.	FAULT TRACING	32
V.	THE TOOL KIT	42
VI.	THE CYCLE PARTS	45
VII.	ROUTINE MAINTENANCE	60
VIII.	MAJOR OVERHAULS	83
IX.	FOR READY REFERENCE	106
	Index	109

CHAPTER I

THE B.S.A./TRIUMPH RANGE

UNDOUBTEDLY the first machine ever designed which was recognizably a motor-scooter was one built for the Danish War Department in 1904. It was an inspiration upon the part of the Danish aviation pioneer, Ellehammer, but there is no record of this machine ever having been marketed as a private venture.

Several other scooter-type machines were produced before, during and after the 1914–18 War—none of them commercially successful. The problems posed by engine, frame and suspension design were, in fact, too formidable to be solved at that relatively early period of transport development.

In 1945, however, the motor-scooter was reborn, almost by accident, when the Italian Piaggio concern built a runabout which could be used by their staff between departments in their huge, but badly damaged, factory at Pontedera. It was so successful that a redesigned version was put into production for general sale, and more than 40 years after Ellehammer's pioneer machine had appeared, the motor-scooter at last became a commercial proposition.

With memories of the short-lived scooter boom of the early '20s still in their minds, British firms were somewhat loth to enter this field, and the major motor-cycle factories were, in any case, heavily committed with both home and export orders for motor-cycles. As a result, British industry was a late starter in the scooter market, but from the early '50s design departments kept an eye on scooter development, and more than one prototype was built. When, at length, a completely British motor-scooter did appear from the motor-cycle industry proper, it was one which was technically well ahead of its international competitors.

This machine was the 250 c.c. B.S.A. "Sunbeam," which is also marketed by Triumph as the "Tigress." It is built to the design of Edward Turner, one of Britain's leading designers in both motor-cycle and automobile engineering, and it was shown in public for the first time at the Earls Court Motorcycle Show late in 1958. A few years later, the range offered by B.S.A. and Triumph was widened by the introduction of a 175 c.c. two-stroke machine using the same cycle parts.

A few details of external finish apart, there is no basic difference between the B.S.A. and Triumph machines. They share an immensely strong frame of part-welded, duplex cradle design, in which the steering head is through-bolted to a pair of large-diameter steel tubes. These frame tubes form the main structure, and are cross-braced at four points, as well as being joined at the top by an elliptical tubular member which forms the seat support. A triangulated sub-frame, of tubular construction, gives added strength at this point, and serves as an upper mounting for the rear suspension's single-spring unit.

The front forks are of radically unconventional design, and are intended to give all the advantages of an overhung front spindle, while retaining the structural rigidity of a conventional fork. This is achieved by using two telescopic members in tandem, the front wheel spindle being carried on a massive cast light-alloy member which comprises a brake back-plate and two heavily-bushed plunger chambers. One of these chambers contains the suspension spring, which is positively located by a through-bolt at each end, while the other serves as an independent hydraulic damping unit.

In the rear suspension, too, the same advantages of easy wheel-changing and structural rigidity have been attained by utilizing the massive, cast light-alloy rear chaincase as the suspension arm, while providing it with two pivot bearings—one on each side of the primary drive gear-case on the engine gearbox unit, the left-hand bearing being carried in a special outrigger casting bolted to the swinging arm.

With this arrangement, the engine/gearbox/suspension unit is offered-up as an entity to the main frame, and an extremely strong structure results.

On the 250 c.c. machine, the engine is a vertical-twin four-stroke. Triumph were the pioneers of this type of engine in its modern form, their "Speed Twin" of 1938 having set the fashion for what has become the most favoured type of motor-cycle in post-War years. It is a design which gives a combination of smooth running and quick throttle response, and since a quite large engine of this type occupies a relatively small space it was ideally suited to a scooter, where the engine has to be contained within a bodywork.

By adopting an "over-square" layout—i.e. by using a cylinder bore which is greater than the stroke—a very compact unit was obtained and, at the same time, piston speeds were kept low, thereby reducing internal wear. Extra sturdiness was gained by casting the cylinders, crankcase and gearbox shell as a one-piece unit—itself quite a creditable technical feat—with cylinder liners of iron alloy also cast into position. A one-piece cylinder head, of light alloy, carries overhead valves, operated by push rods from a single camshaft at the rear of the crankcase compartment.

Of massive design, the crankshaft is of manganese steel, with a large central bob-weight, carried on a copper/lead-alloy bearing on the timing side and a deep-groove ball bearing on the drive side. For the big-end bearings, shell-type liners of steel-backed white metal are employed, and the split connecting rods are of manganese steel. Dry-sump lubrication, with a bolted-on pressed-steel sump, is employed.

Power is transmitted to the gearbox by gears, with a three-plate clutch operating at engine speed. The gearbox is of conventional four-speed design, with positive-stop mechanism for the foot-operated gear control. The final drive is by a duplex chain, with slipper-type tensioner.

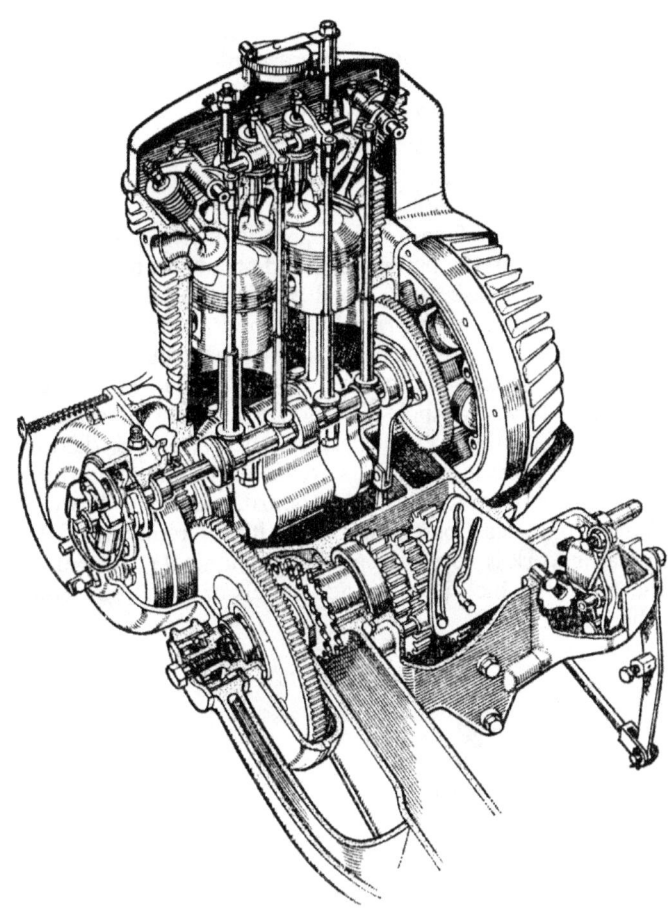

Fig. 1. A Cutaway Drawing of the 250 c.c. Engine
Showing clearly the working parts, which are described in this chapter

Current for ignition and lighting is supplied by an a.c. generator driven at engine speed and mounted on the engine mainshaft. Its external flywheel is provided with vanes, and these are used to pump air through the metal trunking surrounding the engine for cooling purposes.

On the ignition side, separate coils are used for the individual cylinders, and the double-contact-breaker mechanism—which is driven by the camshaft—is equipped with an automatic system for advancing and retarding the spark.

Where a self-starter is fitted, a 12-volt electrical system is used. The starter motor is a separate unit, bolted to a housing in front of the engine, and operating a toothed ring on the flywheel through a Bendix drive. On kick-starter models, the electrical system is rated at 6 volts.

Only one major modification has been made since the introduction of this advanced 250 c.c. scooter. On engines later than No. 16,400 a re-designed exhaust system, with a repositioned silencer, is used. To accommodate this, part of the cooling system was also modified, but from the practical aspect this change has no effect, and the working instructions set out in later chapters still apply.

The same sturdiness of design is apparent in the simpler 175 c.c. two-stroke. Here, although the barrel and head are separate units, the gearbox shell and a half-crankcase are formed as a single casting, and particular attention has been paid to the rigidity of the lower half of the engine by employing four deep-groove ball bearings to carry the shaft. Here, again, overall height is kept to a minimum by use of an "over square" layout.

Both machines have five-inch-diameter front and rear brakes; pressed-steel wheels; and 3·50 in. × 10 in. tyres. Bodywork is identical in each case. Seven basic pressed-steel units are bolted to the main frame to form the front shield and mudguard, footboard, and rear body shell. All routine maintenance can be carried out without removing the panelling, but when major work is necessary all the mechanical parts can be bared by freeing the 10 bolts which join the side panels and the four bolts securing them to the frame.

CHAPTER II

BASIC PRINCIPLES OF THE SCOOTER

ALTHOUGH modern machines are well designed, to obtain the best from them it is essential to know exactly how they work, and why. This applies not only to the maintenance of the machine—important though that is—but also to its actual use on the road.

So far as engines are concerned, there are two basic types in production for scooters today—the four-stroke engine and the two-stroke. In construction they are similar, but the four-stroke is the more efficient. To make it so, however, it has to have a greater number of parts than the two-stroke.

These terms—four-stroke and two-stroke—actually refer to the number of working strokes in one complete cycle of operation of the engine. In the four-stroke engine, then, a working cycle consists of four strokes—in other words, the piston travels from its uppermost position to its lowest, and vice-versa, four times. In an equivalent two-stroke engine, it would make only two such trips.

Before considering just how the engine works, it is necessary to know the names of the major components. First, there is the *cylinder*—which is, as its name implies, simply a metal cylinder. It is closed at one end by a *cylinder head* which, in the case of an overhead-valve four-stroke such as the 250 c.c. B.S.A. and Triumph machines, is equipped with channels (*ports*) through which gas can flow. For each cylinder, there is an *inlet port* and an *exhaust port*. These are closed by *valves*, which are held in the closed position by *valve springs*. To open the valves, a form of mechanical see-saw called a *rocker* is used—one to each valve.

The lower half of the engine consists of a light-alloy case, known as the *crankcase*, on which the cylinder is mounted. Carried on *bearings* inside the crankcase is the *crankshaft*. This shaft may be either a real shaft, or else a pair of heavy *flywheels*, each with its own *half-shaft*, and joined by a *crankpin*. But, though the main shafts are mounted centrally, the crankpin is off-set, so that when the crankshaft is revolved the crankpin moves on a circular path. If, then, the crankpin happened to be at the top of the case, and the crankshaft was revolved, it would not simply rotate, as would the main shafts. Instead, it would move, at first, downwards and forwards. Once the shaft had been rotated through a right angle, the pin would, while still moving downwards, begin to move backwards also. After half a turn, it would begin to move upwards and backwards until, in the last quarter-turn, it moved upwards and forwards.

If, then, a *connecting rod* is attached to a crankpin, the end so fixed would move with the pin in just such a manner. This part of the connecting rod is usually called the *big end*—for the very obvious reason that that particular end of the rod is, invariably, the bigger end.

The other end of the rod, too, has a pin. This is the *gudgeon pin*, and it carries a *piston*, made of light alloy. This piston fits closely in the cylinder, in which it is free to slide up and down. Split-cast iron *piston rings* fixed in *grooves* on the piston ensure a gas-tight seal.

If, in this basic engine, the piston is at the top of its travel it is said to be at *top dead centre*—a term usually abbreviated to t.d.c. If it is right at the

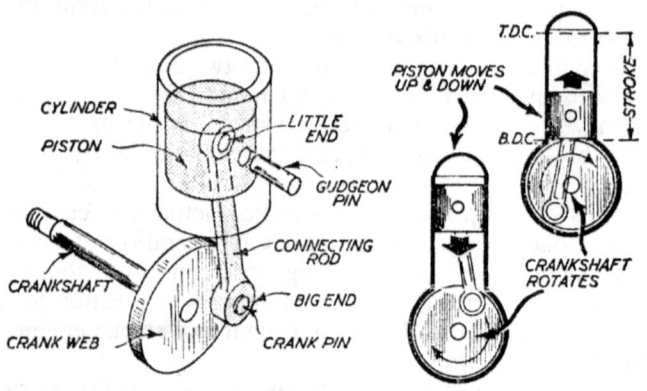

FIG. 2. THE BASIC PARTS OF A SINGLE-CYLINDER INTERNAL COMBUSTION ENGINE

bottom of its travel, it is at *bottom dead centre*, or b.d.c. The distance it must travel between these two points is called the *stroke*, and this is normally measured in millimetres. The B.S.A. and Triumph "250s," for example, have a stroke of 50.62 mm.

To understand the four-stroke cycle, imagine that the piston is now at t.d.c., and that the crankshaft is revolving. As it does so, the crankpin moves, at first, downwards and forwards. This means that the big end of the connecting rod must also move downwards and forwards. Since connecting rods cannot stretch, it exerts a pull on the gudgeon pin, and this in turn pulls the piston downwards. The piston being, of course, a close fit in the bore, is unable to move forwards or backwards. It can only travel up and down.

As the piston moves down the cylinder, the valve which had been closing the inlet port is opened. Inside the cylinder, the movement of the piston has lowered the pressure so that it is below that of the air outside, and air therefore starts to flow through the inlet port into the cylinder. On its way, earlier, it was mixed with petrol to form a mixture which can be burned.

BASIC PRINCIPLES OF THE SCOOTER

This induction of combustible mixture continues for the whole period during which the piston is travelling down the cylinder, and this stroke is consequently called the *induction stroke*.

After half a revolution of the crankshaft, the downward movement of the piston ends, since the crankpin must now begin to press the connecting rod upwards. Obviously, if the inlet port were to be left open, all the mixture which had just been induced would simply be blown out again, and the valve is, therefore, so arranged that it closes at about this point. The rising piston now compresses the mixture, and this gives the second stroke of the cycle—the *compression stroke*.

By the time the piston reaches t.d.c. on this stroke, the mixture in the cylinder has been squeezed into the tiny *combustion chamber* formed between the top of the piston—the *crown*—and the inside surface of the cylinder head. On a scooter, this chamber will have a volume only about one-seventh that of the cylinder itself. The ratio between this and the *swept volume*—the amount of mixture induced into the engine—is called the *compression ratio*, and this is one of the vital factors in deciding the characteristics of an engine. In the case quoted, here, the compression ratio would be 7 to 1. If the mixture had been compressed into one tenth of its original volume it would have been 10 to 1.

Once the gas has been so compressed, it is ready to be burned. A spark occurs, and this ignites the mixture, which burns rapidly. In doing so, it expands, so that it can no longer be contained within the tiny combustion chamber. It exerts pressure upon every surface around it—but, of these, only one can move. This is the piston crown, and the effect of igniting the mixture is to create a pressure inside the combustion chamber which thrusts the piston down the cylinder on the third of its four strokes—the *power stroke*. This time, there is no question of the piston being *pulled* down by the crankpin. On the power stroke, it is the piston which thrusts the connecting rod down. And the rod, in turn, causes the crankpin to revolve, thereby turning the flywheels and rotating the *main shafts*. These, in turn, drive the vehicle through the medium of *gears* and *chains*.

One further stroke remains to complete the cycle—the *exhaust stroke*. When the piston reaches b.d.c. the driving force behind it is largely spent, and it now remains to clear the burned gases out of the cylinder. Carried by the momentum stored in the *flywheels*, the piston starts to rise. As it does so, the second valve in the cylinder head—the *exhaust valve*—is opened. The rising piston pushes the burned gases up the cylinder and out of the exhaust port. At about t.d.c., the exhaust valve again closes the port; the inlet valve opens; the piston begins to descend once more; fresh mixture is induced—and another cycle of operations has begun.

That, then, gives us the basic four-stroke cycle—Induction, Compression, Power, Exhaust. Induction and Power are downward strokes; Compression and Exhaust upward strokes.

With the two-stroke engine, however, all this is re-arranged to occur in only two strokes. The object is to give a smoother-running engine by arranging for a power stroke to occur each time the piston travels from t.d.c. to b.d.c., whereas the four-stroke fires only on alternate downward strokes. Also, the two-stroke is intended to provide an altogether simpler sort of engine. Like the four-stroke, it has a crankcase, crankshaft,

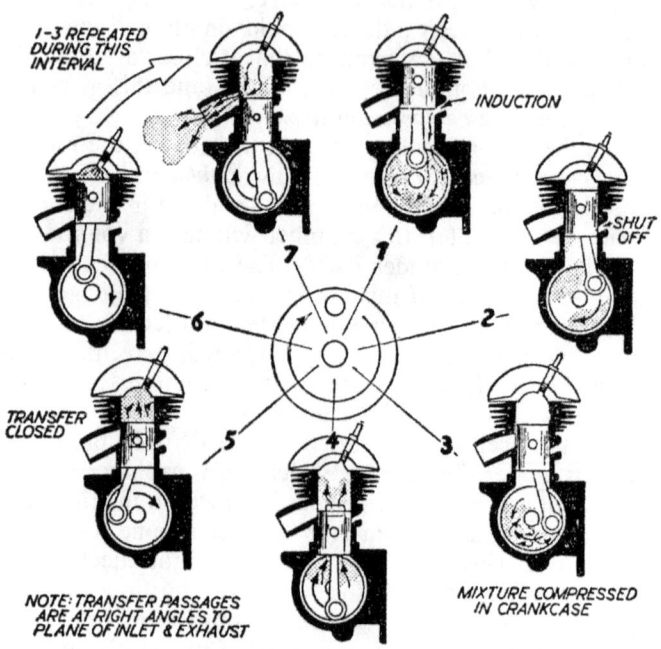

Fig. 3. The Two-stroke Cycle

cylinder, piston and cylinder head—but it has none of the complicated valve gear necessary to make a four-stroke work.

Paradoxically, although it is so much simpler in construction, it is less simple in its manner of operation, since there are always at least two things happening at once.

This stems from the fact that the mixture is not, in the first instance, induced straight into the cylinder, but instead enters the crankcase, which is made specially gas-tight for this purpose. Since there are no valves, all the mixture is distributed through ports which are covered and uncovered by the movement of the piston, and these are consequently located at the base of the cylinder, instead of being placed in the cylinder head.

Imagine a two-stroke engine in which the piston is at b.d.c. after a power stroke. At this moment, the last remnants of the burned gas will still be streaming out of the exhaust port in the side of the cylinder, and two streams of fresh gas entering through a pair of opposed *transfer ports*.

These connect the crankcase with the cylinder, and are placed opposite one another, so that as the two gas streams enter the cylinder they collide and deflect each other upwards, away from the exhaust port.

The piston now begins to travel up the cylinder. First, its upper edge covers the transfer ports, sealing the crankcase. Almost immediately, it then closes the exhaust port, and the cylinder is sealed. The rising piston now begins to compress the fresh charge trapped in the cylinder, in exactly the same way as in the four-stroke engine.

As the piston nears t.d.c., its lower edge (*skirt*) uncovers the inlet port, and a new charge is drawn into the crankcase. At t.d.c., a spark occurs in the combustion chamber, and the piston is thrust down the cylinder on a power stroke. As it descends, it first covers the inlet port with its skirt, and the underside of the piston then begins to compress the mixture in the crankcase. Towards the end of the stroke, the top edge of the piston uncovers the exhaust port, and the burned gases are carried through it by their own momentum. A split second later, the top of the piston uncovers the transfer ports, and the underside of the piston begins to pump the fresh charge out of crankcase, through the transfer ports and into the cylinder.

When considering the working cycle of the two-stroke, therefore, it is necessary to take into account not only what is happening in the cylinder, but also what is taking place simultaneously in the crankcase. Each downward stroke of the piston is a power stroke in the cylinder and a compression stroke in the crankcase. Each upward stroke of the piston is a compression stroke in the cylinder and an induction stroke in the crankcase. There is no exhaust stroke, this being replaced by a mere phase at the tail-end of the power stroke, and the same holds true for the induction stroke, so far as the cylinder is concerned, for this is replaced by the transfer period as the piston approaches b.d.c.

Obviously, when an engine is running at a speed which may reach 5,000 revolutions every minute, there is very little time in which to perform this vital job of clearing the burned gas out of the cylinder and replacing it with fresh gas. When, as in the two-stroke, one attempts to cram all this "breathing" into a few milli-seconds at the end of a stroke some degree of efficiency is bound to be lost—and this, in fact, is precisely what happens.

Since the two-stroke has twice as many power impulses in a given time as the four-stroke, it might be thought that it would develop twice the power from a given size of cylinder. In practice, it often develops slightly less power than the equivalent four-stroke.

One of the reasons is that, at the higher engine speeds, there is this drastically-restricted time in which the engine can "breathe." Another reason lies in the construction of the engine itself. The exhaust port *has* to be opened first, and it follows that if the port is piston-controlled it must therefore close *last*. Consequently, it remains open for a short period when the transfers are closed and the piston is ascending. Inevitably, some of the fresh mixture which has just been induced is expelled through the exhaust port and lost.

Where the two-stroke gains is at low engine speeds—the part of the range where it has more time to "breathe." Here, its actual pulling power (*torque*) is usually greater than that of its four-stroke equivalent, and in some cases this superiority is so pronounced that the two-stroke engine is able to be operated in conjunction with a three-speed gearbox where the four-stroke would call for a more complicated four-speed box.

A vertical-twin engine such as that used in the 250 c.c. B.S.A. and Triumph scooters can be regarded as, virtually, two single-cylinder four-stroke engines coupled together on a common crankshaft. Both pistons rise and fall together—not, as one might expect, alternately. The reason for this is that only in this way can even firing intervals be obtained with a two-cylinder four-stroke engine. In fact, the vertical-twin four-stroke gives exactly the same firing interval as the single-cylinder two-stroke.

As was mentioned earlier, the two-stroke also saves on complication in the actual engine. The valves of a four-stroke have to be operated mechanically, and the usual layout is to arrange for a *shaft* bearing a pair of *cams* for each cylinder to be driven, at half engine speed, through a *chain* or by a *train of gears*. The cams bear on barrel-shaped metal *cam-followers*, and these, in turn, press against steel or alloy rods, known as *push rods*. These push rods bear against one end of the *valve rockers*, and the other end of each pivoted rocker is positioned just above the *stem* of the valve.

When the cam revolves, it pushes the follower and rod upwards. This causes one end of the rocker to rise, and the section above the valve stem (the *tappet*) to fall. This presses the valve downwards against the pressure of its spring, and thereby opens the port. When the cam permits the rocker to return to its normal position, the valve spring returns the valve to its seat, thus closing the port tightly.

Another great simplification which the layout of the two-stroke engine permits is the use of *petroil* lubrication. All engines need oil. Not only does it reduce friction, but it also helps to keep the internal surfaces relatively cool.

With a four-stroke, it is necessary to use an independent oiling system, fed by a *pump*, This delivers oil from a *sump* or *oil tank*, through passageways to bearings, the cylinder walls, and the valve gear. This is, of course, highly efficient, but it calls for the pump itself, its auxiliary drive, an oil container, filters, drain plugs, and passageways.

The two-stroke, however, has its mixture delivered into the crankcase first. If oil is mixed with this fuel, it means that it can be taken into the case and distributed over the bearings and moving parts without any mechanical complication at all. Furthermore, oily mixture is also fed straight into the cylinder from the crankcase, thus giving continual cylinder-wall oiling—by the incoming mixture on the piston's cylinder compression stroke, and by the transfer period at the end of the power stroke.

Crude though it may appear at first glance, the petroil system works well in practice, and it has the added advantage that when climbing hills the engine receives an adequate supply of oil, since the amount induced is proportional to throttle opening, and not merely to engine speed. On the other hand, when descending a hill with the throttle closed the two-stroke can be partially starved of oil, although enough has usually condensed on to the crankcase walls to form an in-built reserve which off-sets this slight disadvantage.

THE CARBURETTOR

We noted, in passing, that when air is induced into the cylinder it is mixed with petrol to form a combustible mixture. This, of course, is a drastic understatement of the magnitude of the job performed by a simple, but precision-engineered, instrument known as the *carburettor*.

In principle, this is little more than a glorified scent-spray with a Gallic name, but it has to carry out one of the most crucial of all jobs—metering out an exact and minute ration of petrol and mixing it thoroughly with air in just the right proportion to enable it to be burned efficiently.

At first sight, this may not appear to be over-exacting, since the ideal ratio is around one part of petrol to 14 parts of air. This, however, is the proportion by *weight*; the carburettor operates by *volume*, and on this basis each 100 c.c. of combustible mixture needs to contain only about 0·2 c.c. of petrol, the remaining 99·8 c.c. being air. Obviously, the carburettor, despite its simplicity, is a precision instrument, and has to be treated accordingly.

The basic components of a carburettor are a petrol reservoir, called a *float chamber*; a *venturi*, or *choke*, through which air is drawn; *jets*, which meter the petrol; and a *throttle*, which controls the amount of mixture passing through the carburettor and into the engine.

Consider, first, the basic method of operation. Petrol is fed to the float chamber. This is very much like a pocket edition of the familiar domestic cistern. The chamber contains a *float*, which rises as petrol is admitted through a valve. In rising the float carries with it a *tapered needle*, and this needle is carefully contoured to fit in a seat in the valve. When the level of petrol in the chamber is correct, the needle is pressed fully home on its seating, thus cutting off the flow of petrol. When the level in the chamber falls the float falls with it, and so does the needle. Leaving its seating, it thus permits more fuel to flow into the chamber, until the correct level is again reached.

Connecting the float chamber with the body of the carburettor is a drilled passageway, through which petrol flows into a *jet well*. A tube is placed vertically in this well, so that its lower end is immersed, while the upper end opens into the venturi. Screwed to the bottom of this tube is a *jet*—an essential part of the carburettor which looks suspiciously like a small screw or bolt with a hole drilled through the centre. That, in fact, is just what it is—but the hole is so proportioned that it will pass just the right amount of fuel, and no more.

When the induction stroke begins in the cylinder, air is drawn through the carburettor venturi, which is so shaped that there is a fall in pressure in the section around the jet tube—called the *mixing chamber*. As a result, petrol is drawn up the tube into the chamber, where it mixes with the air, and passes through the inlet port into the cylinder.

Obviously, a carburettor which consisted of these parts alone would work, but the engine would run at only one speed. Some means of varying the supply of mixture has to be arranged, and this means has to be one which keeps the essential petrol/air proportion correct at all openings.

On scooters, the solution usually adopted is to use a *needle jet* to control the fuel flow into the mixing chamber, and couple this to a *throttle slide* to vary the amount of air admitted.

The jet tube is, therefore, tapered internally to match a long, tapered needle, arranged to move inside it. At the top, this needle is clipped to the *throttle slide*, which is itself capable of moving up and down in the carburettor. A cable, connected to the throttle control, pulls it upwards, and a light spring helps to return it when the control is slackened.

At the front of the slide a half-moon-shaped area is cut away, and it is this *cut-away* which governs the characteristics of the slide, and decides how much air can pass through it at intermediate throttle openings.

When the throttle is closed, only a very small amount of air can pass—so small, in fact, that it is impossible for the main jet to meter out the tiny amount of fuel required. For running under these conditions a very fine jet, called the *pilot jet* delivers a minute ration of petrol to the mixing chamber, and in the main jet itself the throttle needle is hard against its seating, and no petrol at all passes through.

As the throttle is opened, the slide is raised, and so is the needle. More air passes through the venturi, and the movement of the tapered needle opens up a passage for petrol through the main jet. Further movement of the throttle increases both the amount of air permitted to pass and the amount of fuel which the jet supplies, until at full throttle both passages are supplying the maximum amounts of which they are capable.

Since the proper operation of the carburettor depends upon the action of very fine metering devices, great attention is paid to ensuring that the internals are kept free from dirt. Even a speck of dirt is quite enough to block the jet, and thus prevent fuel passing through it. The petrol is, therefore, normally filtered at several points by passing it through fine wire mesh. One such filter is usually fitted around the inlet of the petrol tap, in the fuel tank, and a second filter is placed immediately in front of the float chamber needle valve.

When an engine is cold, it needs a somewhat "richer" mixture than usual to enable it to start, and to supply this it is usual to employ a *strangler*—sometimes called, rather misleadingly, a *choke*. This should not, of course, be confused with the *venturi*.

The purpose of a strangler is to cut down the air supply independently of the petrol supply, thus giving the same amount of fuel but mixing it with a smaller supply of air, and a rich-mixture device of this type is invariably some form of plate which is used to block the carburettor inlet. It can be a supplementary slide; a plate which swings over the mouth of the carburettor; or even a form of shutter on the carburettor air filter.

On the Zenith carburettor fitted to the B.S.A. and Triumph twins, however, a different type of rich-mixture control is employed—a two-position slide through which a by-pass of air continually flows. In one position, this air passes through a large hole; in the other, only a small hole is presented to the airflow, and the total volume of air entering the carburettor is correspondingly reduced. This system is more efficient than one in which the main airflow is interrupted.

Most carburettors, besides being equipped with petrol filters, also have a filter for the air. This is not so much to protect the carburettor as to protect the engine, since the air usually contains dust, and dust—harmless though it may look—comprises a surprising number of very hard particles which are quite capable of scratching the working parts of the engine very badly indeed.

An air filter itself forms an obstacle to the airflow, and cuts the amount of air entering the carburettor. In the design stage, this obstruction is taken into consideration, and the fuel is metered accordingly. If, therefore, an instrument which is intended to have an air filter is used without one, the effect is to weaken the resulting mixture, since more air is entering while the fuel supply remains unaltered. Damage to the internal parts of the engine apart, this is one reason why the engine should not be run with the air filter removed.

THE IGNITION SYSTEM

Even really experienced riders often have only the slightest knowledge of the working of the electrical system, upon which the whole operation of the engine depends. As a result, the electrics are frequently neglected; failure results; and the immediate conclusion is that electricity is thoroughly unreliable anyway!

There is no need, however, to be a qualified electrical engineer to understand *how* the system works, even if the actual reasons behind it have to be taken for granted.

All electrical practice is founded upon *circuits* and upon the fact that an electric current will invariably take the shortest path to earth. In this connexion, though, it should be emphasized that "earth" does not necessarily mean the ground. So far as a scooter's electrical system is concerned, "earth" is the mass of the scooter itself—a little world which is all its own.

A circuit is just what its name implies. In this, electricity is rather like a model railway train. If all the points are correctly set, the train will go round and round. If they are not so set, it will simply end up standing still on a siding.

As with the train, so with electricity. Providing there is a circuit, the current will flow. If the circuit is broken, it will not. And, just occasionally, there may be some bad points setting which directs it straight to earth—a *short circuit*—just as if the train had been directed on to a branch line leading straight to the edge of a cliff. . . .

Electricity is measured in *volts* and *amperes*. The *volt* is a measure of its force; the *ampere* basically a measure of the number of electrons per second passing a given point. A current of one ampere is one in which 6,300,000,000,000,000,000 electrons per second pass the point. In other words, while *voltage* indicates the electrical pressure in the circuit, *amperes* indicate the *quantity* of electricity which is flowing. The resistance to the flow presented by the wires and so forth which make up the circuit is measured in *Ohms*, one ohm being a resistance which calls for one volt to be applied so that one ampere may flow.

Electricity is further regarded as comprising two basic types of current—*positive* and *negative*—but for all practical purposes it is only necessary to know that these do, in fact, exist.

Finally, it is necessary to accept one further basic fact—that when a *coil* is placed in a magnetic field electricity is produced.

Two types of machine for producing electricity are used on engines, the *a.c. generator* and the *d.c. generator*. The first produces a form of current which *alternates*, producing a constantly reversing flow. The second produces direct current, which flows in one direction only.

On the 250 c.c. machines, an a.c. generator is used. On the 175 c.c. machine a d.c. flywheel magneto-generator is employed.

In such a design permanent magnets are mounted inside the rim of the external flywheel, and a stator plate, bolted to the engine, holds an ignition coil and lighting coils, each being simply closely-wound coils of fine wire. They are different, however, in that the ignition coil is really two coils in one—a low-tension *primary winding* surrounding a high-tension *secondary winding*, but fully insulated from it.

There is one other essential part—the *contact-breaker*. This is simply a mechanical switch, consisting of a pair of points which are opened and closed by a cam carried on the engine mainshaft. Electrically, the contact-breaker is connected into the low-tension side of the ignition circuit.

From the high-tension part of the coil, a heavily-insulated *high-tension lead* is connected to a *sparking plug*, set in the cylinder head. This plug consists of a *body*, which screws into the head, and an insulated *central electrode* to which the high-tension lead is connected. Welded to the body is a *side electrode*—some plugs may have several—which is set so that a gap of around 20 thousandths of an inch exists between its tip and that of the central electrode.

When the flywheel is revolved, the magnets set up a magnetic field, and low-tension electricity is generated in the primary winding of the ignition coil. At a pre-determined point, however, the cam presses one of the points of the contact-breaker away from the other, and thus breaks the circuit.

Here something happens which has to be taken on trust. This sudden rupturing of the low-tension circuit in the primary winding of the ignition coil creates a high-tension current in the coil's secondary winding. This current is of very high voltage—around 33,000 volts, which is the same as that carried in the conductors of the rural electricity grid system. Seeking the shortest path to earth, this current streaks down the high-tension lead. Normally it would stop dead at the gap in the sparking plug, but the pressure behind it is too great to permit it to do so. Instead, it jumps across the gap in the form of a hot, blue spark, and it is this spark which ignites the mixture in the cylinder. In a normal scooter two-stroke engine, this operation can occur some 5,000 times every minute.

To prevent the low-tension current from doing at the contact-breaker points just what the high-tension current subsequently does at the sparking plug gap—jumping across in the form of a spark—a small electrical "shock-absorber," called a *condenser* is added to the circuit.

With the a.c. system the principle is similar, but the actual mechanics of the operation are different. Instead of the current being supplied from the generator, the primary windings are energized from a battery, and the battery is itself kept charged by the generator. Since direct current is needed for charging, the alternating current is passed, first, through a *rectifier*, which is a form of electrical non-return valve, permitting current to pass in one direction only, and thereby converting the a.c. supplied by the generator into d.c. for battery-charging.

The lighting systems and horn are supplied with electricity from the battery in both cases.

THE TRANSMISSION

Internal-combustion motors are high-speed engines, in which power output is, within limits, proportional to the speed of rotation of the engine. At low speeds, therefore, less power is developed than at high speeds. Where outside factors, such as a hill, increase the load on the engine its speed—and, consequently, its power—falls off. This, in turn, reduces its speed still further, causing a further drop in power. At length, the load becomes so great than it overcomes the remaining power of the engine and the motor "stalls."

Basically, there is a comparatively narrow range of engine speed at which the greatest power is developed, and the engine should, ideally, run at this speed wherever possible. The designer does, in fact, try to arrange for this maximum power to occur at cruising speed.

To deal with varying loads, however, some means of keeping the engine speed up when the road speed falls is necessary, and this need is met by the *gearbox*.

This consists, basically, of an *input* and *output shaft*, on which are carried a series of meshing *gears*. Each pair of gears gives a different reduction between the speeds of the two shafts. Only one pair of gears can be used to transmit the power at any one time, and in the B.S.A. and Triumph scooters a choice of four different gear ratios is provided.

Initially, the *primary drive*, which transmits the crankshaft movement to the gearbox, provides the first reduction in speed—cutting the rotational speed by approximately one half. This is reduced still further in the gearbox itself, depending upon which pair of gears is locked into position on the shafts, and there is a further reduction between the gearbox and the rear wheel in the *secondary transmission*. In top gear, therefore, the engine crankshaft will revolve four times for each revolution of the rear wheel, but in bottom gear it will turn over 12 times. In one revolution of the rear wheel, then, top gear allows the force of two power strokes to be applied, but in bottom gear—in the same distance covered—the power of six strokes is passed through to the driving wheel. Thus an increase in load can be counter-balanced by changing into a lower gear, and bringing more power to bear in a given distance, at the cost of a drop in road speed.

The method employed to lock the various gears to the shafts is supremely simple. Certain gears are free to revolve on the shafts, and others revolve with the shaft, but are free to slide sideways on *splines*. Castellations on the side faces of the gears—*dogs*—enable adjacent gears to be coupled together when a sliding gear is moved sideways by a *selector fork*. Selector fork movement, in turn, is controlled by a *quadrant*, in the face of which are cut slots, which form *cams*. Movement of this quadrant causes pegs to move in the cam slots, and this movement is transmitted to the selectors.

A vital part of the transmission is the *clutch*, which enables the drive to be freed at will. A clutch consists of one disc member driven by the engine; a drum member which is connected to the transmission; and friction plates which link the two, together with springs and a withdrawal mechanism.

On the B.S.A. and Triumph twins, the main body of the clutch carrying one of the two gears of the primary drive, is free to rotate upon the engine mainshaft. Splined to the mainshaft—but not mechanically connected to the clutch body—is the clutch centre.

The clutch centre has a series of splines on its boss, and the clutch body a series of splines around its inner periphery. Inside, fit a pressure plate and a series of six clutch plates. Three of these carry friction linings, and are splined around the outer edge to match the splining of the clutch body. They have, however, no internal splines to join them to the clutch centre.

BASIC PRINCIPLES OF THE SCOOTER

Fitted alternately with these lined plates are three plain steel plates. These *are* internally splined to match the clutch centre, but have no peripheral splines to join them to the clutch body.

Three strong springs, held by a spring plate, press these plates hard together. When the clutch centre is driven by the crankshaft it turns, carrying with it the three plain plates. Owing to the pressure exerted by the springs, the friction between these and the lined plates is such that they also turn as one unit with the plain plates, and in so doing rotate the clutch body and transmit the drive.

When the withdrawal mechanism is operated, the pressure of the springs is relieved. The clutch centre and the plates fixed to it still revolve, but the friction between these and the lined plates is now too low to transmit movement. The lined plates therefore remain stationary, and so does the clutch body. No drive is transmitted.

By gradually releasing the withdrawal mechanism, the revolving plain plates can be brought into gradual contact with the lined plates. At first, these slip, but as contact is increased they speed up, until with the full spring pressure restored the whole clutch is once again rotating as a complete unit. This is what happens each time the scooter moves off from a standstill.

STEERING, SUSPENSION AND BRAKES

When a scooter is driven along a road, it remains upright for exactly the same reason that a gyroscope refuses to topple over—the two revolving wheels do, in effect, act as a pair of gyroscopes, and resist attempts to force them out of their course.

There are, however, other factors which enter into it. One is the design of the steering gear. This is so arranged that—although the fact is not immediately apparent—the front wheel is trailing, rather like the castor of an armchair. The characteristics of the steering depend to some extent upon the amount of *trail* specified by the designer, and to some extent upon other factors. One of these is the *rake*—the angle at which the steering head is set—and others are the weight distribution of the machine as a whole and the position of its centre of gravity.

In addition, the manner in which the suspension systems act plays a great part in determining whether the scooter handles well or not. The B.S.A./Triumph design utilizes a telescopic front fork, in which a plunger carrying the wheel moves upwards and backwards, sliding up the fork leg against the resistance of a spring. This movement has to be *damped*—if there were no damper, the spring would thrust the wheel up and down with a rapid action, and so cause the front end of the machine to pitch up and down.

To prevent this, a *hydraulic damper* is used. This consists of an oil chamber, formed in the sliding member, and a disc valve screwed into the end of the fixed fork leg. This valve is so designed that when the sliding member rises it permits the oil to pass through into the fork leg with little or no resistance. On the return stroke, the valve is partially closed, and this slows down the rate at which the oil can return to the chamber in the sliding member. Passing through the centre of the valve is a steel rod, fixed to the sliding member. This is topped by a washer, operating inside the fork leg and closely fitted to it—rather like the leather washer inside a tyre pump.

This washer which naturally moves with the sliding member, has its rate of return slowed by the oil trapped in the fork leg between the bottom of the washer and the top of the disc valve, and in consequence the return stroke of the sliding member is also slowed down, thereby preventing spring oscillation. A similar layout is adopted at the rear, where the suspension is controlled by a large coil spring, which surrounds an independent hydraulic damper.

Just as important as making the scooter move is the ability to make it stop. This is the job of the brakes, which are of the internal-expanding type. Each wheel carries a *drum*, the inside surfaces of which are accurately ground so that the drum is completely round and true.

Closing the drum is a *back-plate*, and affixed to this plate is a *pivot pin*. Diametrically opposed to the pin is a cam, which is connected to the brake lever.

Two *brake-shoes*—semi-circular in shape, with a friction lining riveted to the outer curve on each shoe—are fitted with one end butting on the pivot pin and the other on one face of the cam. They are held together by a spring, and the whole back-plate assembly is fixed rigidly to the machine.

When the brake lever or pedal is operated, the cam turns and presses the free ends of the shoes outwards. This brings the friction linings into contact with the inside surfaces of the drum, decelerating the machine.

A brake is basically a form of heat-exchanger. The friction created by the linings rubbing on the surface of the drum absorbs energy which would otherwise be devoted to driving the scooter, and this energy is converted into heat, which is dissipated from the surface of the drum.

Both brakes on the B.S.A./Triumph machines are controlled by cables. In addition, cables are used for the throttle, clutch and choke controls. For efficient operation, a cable depends upon the correct relationship between its inner and outer wires being maintained. Since the inner wires have a tendency to stretch, the outer casings are provided with screwed adjusters, which in effect enable the effective length of the outer casing to be varied in relation to the inner wire. All cables work against the resistance of a spring, by which the return action is supplied, since cables normally perform well only when used in tension.

CHAPTER III

HANDLING SCOOTERS

IF a novice were asked to step into an aeroplane and fly away with no instruction beyond being shown the controls he would refuse, point-blank. Yet the novice who buys a scooter is often expected to find out for himself just how to ride the machine, despite the fact that he is serving his novitiate on the most crowded roads in Europe, if not in the world.

Of course, a scooter is relatively easy to handle, and it is also an inherently safe type of vehicle, but the fact remains that teaching oneself is definitely not the ideal way to learn any art. To this, the art of riding a scooter is no exception.

In some parts of the country, it is possible to enrol for a course in the R.A.C./A.-C.U. Learner Training Scheme. This is an excellent series of a dozen riding lessons, arranged to fill a twelve-week course, In addition, there are 12 lectures. The instruction is given by skilled riders who are members of A.-C.U. clubs, and in the initial stages training takes place on private property. Only when the instructor feels that his pupil has sufficient confidence and knowledge is open road work included.

At the end of the course, a successful pupil is fully trained, and is eligible to undergo the Proficiency Test as a prelude to his Ministry of Transport driving test. As yet, the Proficiency Certificate itself is not accepted as a substitute for the M.o.T. Test.

Unfortunately, not all parts of the country are covered by the Training Scheme, but it is being constantly expanded, and The Manager, R.A.C. Motorcycle Dept., 85 Pall Mall, London, S.W.1, is always prepared to put interested riders in touch with his nearest local training centre.

Where no Training Scheme Centre is available, self-tuition unfortunately has to fill the gap. At this stage, it is essential not to form bad habits, which become very difficult indeed to break. The riding style which the learner evolves during this formative stage of his roadfaring is going to determine not only whether he becomes a safe and skilful rider, but also how much strain he places upon his machine. Much wear and tear, and a considerable amount of time-wasting mechanical tinkering, can be saved by riding habits alone, providing they are good ones!

As a first step, an afternoon should be spent in an armchair, studying this chapter and learning exactly how all the controls are set out and operated. Obviously, the first step in riding a scooter is to start the engine, so the first group of controls to be considered are those for the petrol, ignition, and the engine. The petrol tap is situated inside the bodywork, and can only be reached by operating the catch, on the right-hand side of the scooter, which locks the dualseat. When this catch is pulled out the seat can be hinged sideways. The tap itself is mounted on the front of the petrol tank, and is operated by an extension rod. To switch on the fuel, the rod is pulled upwards. If the fuel is very low, it may be necessary to use the reserve supply, which is brought into operation by twisting the

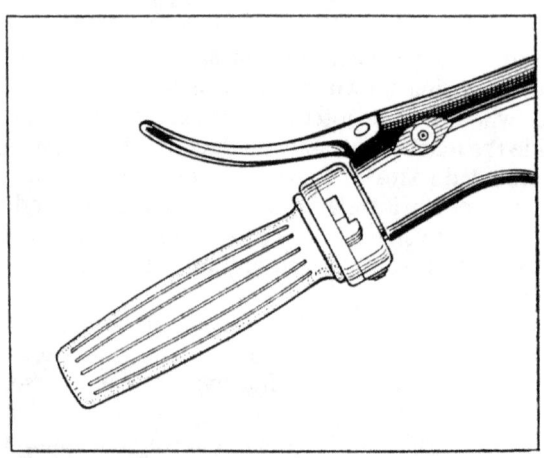

FIG. 4. THE CLUTCH LEVER ON THE LEFT HANDLEBAR
Mounted beside the dummy twist-grip, in a barrel-shaped housing, is the dip switch for the headlamp and the push-button horn control. The 175 c.c. model also has an ignition cut-out button to stop the engine.

tap knob in a clockwise direction and pulling it at the same time. After a run, the fuel should always be turned off.

No ignition switch is fitted to the 175 c.c. machine, but on the 250 c.c. model one is located on the left-hand side of the instrument panel. It is a three-position switch, and for normal starting the knob should be turned to the right, to bring the "IGN" marking opposite the small indicator line moulded on the panel. The "EMG" position is used only if the battery is flat.

To make cold starting easier, all B.S.A. and Triumph machines are fitted with choke controls, which give a richer mixture when operated. The choke knob is on the left-hand side of the "backbone," just beneath the instrument panel. It should be pulled out when making the first start of the day, and it may be necessary to use it at other times if the engine fails to start promptly.

Once the engine is running, the choke control should be pressed home again. It may, however, be necessary to leave the choke in operation for, say, the first half-mile on really cold days.

On the right handlebar is the throttle control—a twist grip, which is turned towards the rider to increase engine speed, and away from the rider to decrease engine speed. Its action is natural, and very sensitive.

One further control is involved in starting—the kick starter pedal, which is mounted alongside the right footboard. With the fuel turned on, the choke knob pulled out, and the ignition on, the starting routine involves nothing more complicated than making sure that the scooter has not been left in gear, and then depressing the kick starter with the foot. Although

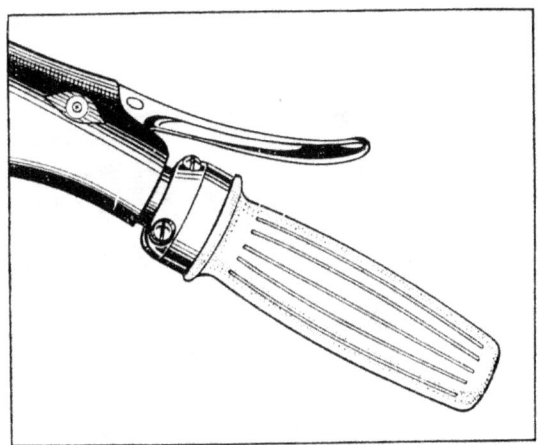

FIG. 5. TWO CONTROLS ARE MOUNTED ON THE RIGHT HANDLEBAR
The twist-grip is the throttle control, which is turned towards the rider to open the throttle. The lever controls the front brake.

it is *called* a kick starter it is not, in fact, kicked. The correct action is to press it down smartly with the foot, increasing the pressure all the way, so that the crankshaft is revolved quickly several times.

Sometimes even use of the choke does not give quite a rich enough mixture, and there is one further method of feeding extra petrol to the engine. The seat is lifted, and the small button on top of the carburettor float chamber is depressed, and held down for about five seconds. This button is called a tickler. It merely holds the carburettor float down, and thus allows an extra flow of petrol to reach the jet. Care should be taken not to misuse the tickler by holding it down for more than a few seconds. Too rich a mixture can result, and this is almost impossible to ignite.

Once the engine has been started the obvious next step is to go somewhere—which is where the clutch and gear controls come in! Before the gears can be engaged the clutch must be disengaged, and this is done merely by pulling the clutch lever—mounted on the left handlebar—right back to the bar. The gear pedal, which is the front pedal on the right side of the footboard—is then pressed forward with the foot to engage first gear, and the clutch released to take up the drive.

Subsequent gear changes are made by closing the throttle, withdrawing the clutch, and moving the gear lever backwards or forwards as the case may be. A positive-stop change is provided—which means that the gear pedal can be moved only one step at a time. From neutral, pressing the pedal forwards engages first gear. When it is pulled backwards for the first time it selects second gear. Third gear is obtained by pulling it

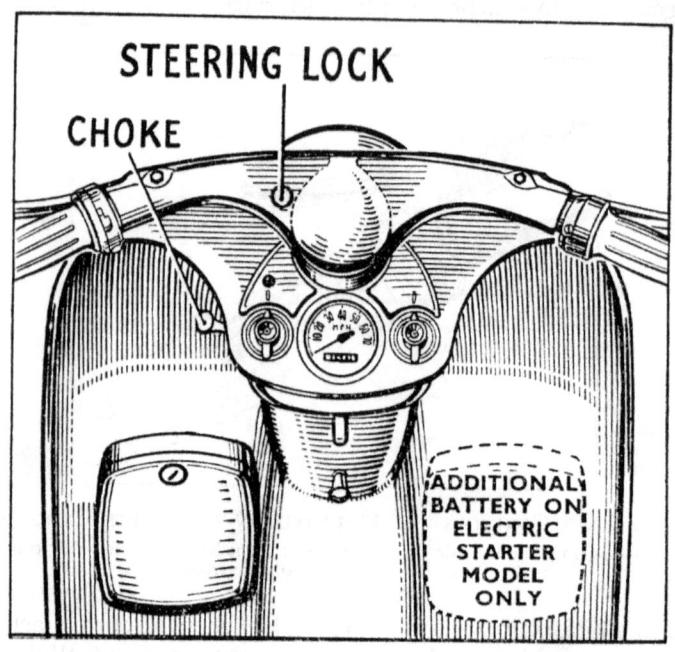

FIG. 6. THE INSTRUMENT PANEL ON THE 250 C.C. MACHINE

This contains two switches and the speedometer; the choke button is mounted on the shielding and the handlebar fairing contains a steering lock. A similar layout—apart from the switches—is used on the 175 c.c. model.

backwards again; fourth gear by yet another backward movement. Each time the pedal moves just far enough to engage the requisite gear, and when released springs back to its normal, central position. It is, therefore, necessary to remember which gear is engaged—which is not one quarter as difficult as it sounds. This type of gearchange is fast and accurate.

A pedal mounted well back on the right of the footboard is the neutral selector. This is used to "find" neutral easily from second gear. With second gear engaged, it is only necessary to pull out the clutch and press the heel firmly on the neutral selector pedal to disengage gear easily. The pedal should not be violently kicked, but merely tapped with the heel when resistance is felt to its movement.

Two of the most important controls on the machine are those for the brakes. The front brake is the more powerful of the two, and it is controlled by a lever fitted to the right handlebar. The further this lever is pulled towards the rider the harder the brake is applied. A pedal on the left of the footboard controls the rear brake. It is essential that *both* controls should be used together when making a stop.

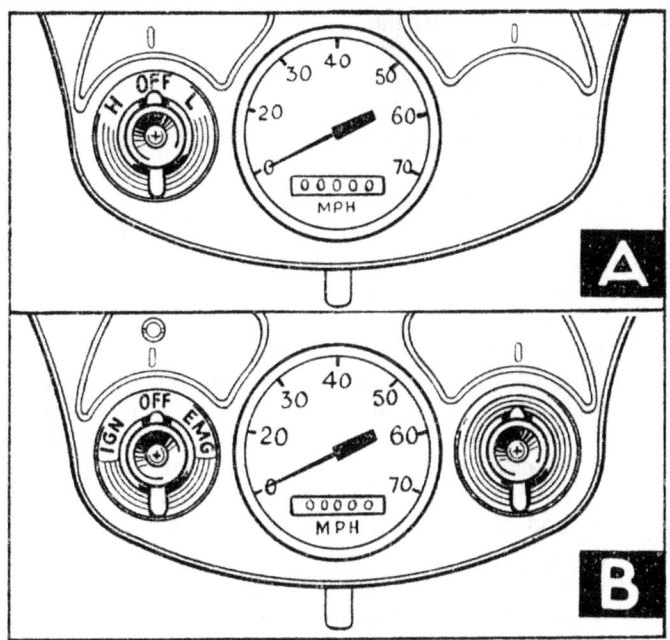

FIG. 7. THE SWITCHGEAR ON THE 175 C.C. MACHINE (A) AND THE INSTRUMENT PANEL ON THE 250 C.C. MACHINE (B)

(A) shows the switchgear in which a single switch is turned to H for the headlamp or to L for the parking light. There is no ignition switch.
(B) shows the left-hand switch which controls the ignition. "Ign" is the position for switching on the ignition; "Emg" is the emergency starting position. The lighting switch, on the right, is turned to the left for the headlamp and to the right for the parking lights.

Near the dummy twist-grip on the left handlebar is a drum equipped with a switch and a push-button. The button controls the horn, and the switch is used to select either the main or the dipped headlamp beam when riding at night, the dipped beam being used, of course, when other traffic approaches. It should also be used for town cruising. On the 175 c.c. model there is also a button which cuts out the ignition and so stops the engine when it is no longer required to tick over.

Controlling the lights themselves is a separate switch, mounted on the left of the instrument panel on 175 c.c. machines, and on the right on 250 c.c. models. The 175 c.c. switch has its positions marked—"H" for the main beam; "L" for the pilot and parking lights. No markings are made on the 250 c.c. machine's switch, which is turned to the left to operate the headlamp and to the right to switch on the parking light.

On the handlebars, just to the left of the centre of the fairing, is a Yale-type lock. This is intended to thiefproof the machine, and it is operated by a key. It has the effect of locking the steering in one position, and should be used whenever the scooter is left unattended.

Where an electric starter is fitted, there is one other control. This is the starter knob, which is fitted centrally on the vertical backbone behind the front shield. The starting routine with an electric starter model is exactly the same as with a kick-starter scooter, save that instead of turning the engine with the kick starter one merely pulls the knob instead. One should not, of course, operate the starter for minutes on end since electric starting places a terrific load on the batteries, which can easily be run flat by prolonged use of the starter. If the engine fails to start within five seconds the knob should be released, and the batteries given ten seconds to recover before the control is operated again.

Once the position, purpose and operation of the controls have been memorized, the next step in learning to ride can be taken. Half an hour should be spent sitting on the machine, operating the various controls, getting their "feel," and learning how to locate them instantly by touch alone, without so much as a single downward glance.

This done, the engine should be started, and some minutes passed in gently opening and closing the throttle, and noting the response of the engine. At this stage, too, the tools can be used for the first time—to adjust the friction screw on the throttle. This should be set so that the throttle still works easily, but does not close itself as soon as the hand is removed from the grip. Usually, the dealer will have adjusted the machine's tick-over, but if the engine tends to "cut out" at low speeds the throttle stop on the carburettor should be adjusted to give a rather faster idling speed.

One of the main difficulties faced by a learner is to master the delicate operation of the clutch which is necessary for moving off. At first, this can be practised by starting the engine, standing astride the machine with both feet firmly planted on the ground, pulling out the clutch, and engaging first gear.

Then, let the clutch lever out by unfolding the fingers of the left hand hand from the *knuckles*—not from the finger joints—so that the lever is partially released. This is a fairly rapid action.

Towards the end of the lever travel, the clutch will begin to take up the drive, and the scooter will start to move forward. Check the release instantly, and then draw the clutch out again, select neutral, and release the clutch fully. This is necessary to enable the clutch to rest. If it is held out of engagement for too long the plates may burn.

This exercise should be repeated some half-dozen times, until it is possible to release the clutch lever quickly and accurately and to check it smoothly as the drive begins to take up. Once this initial movement has been mastered, the art of making a smooth get-away is almost attained.

Choose a quiet stretch of road for your first excursions, and make sure that the road behind you is clear before you set off. Then start the engine, and carry out the same procedure as before. This time, however, open the

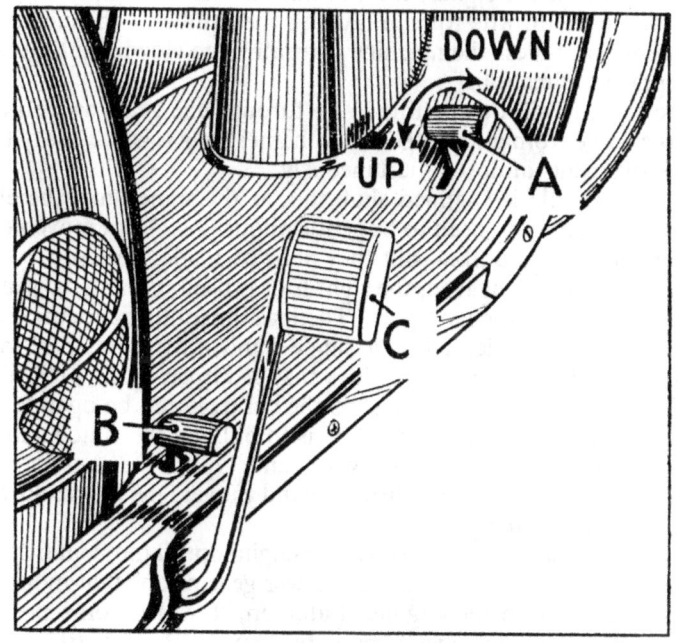

FIG. 8. THE GEARS AND KICK STARTER

The gears are controlled by pedal A. It is pressed forward to select lower gears, and stroked backwards with the foot to select high gears. Pedal B when pressed down will select true neutral from second gear. Pedal C is the kick starter.

throttle, gently, by a fraction of an inch as the clutch "bites," and as the scooter begins to move lift both feet and place them squarely on the footboard.

Simultaneously, unfold the fingers of the left hand—it should take a couple of seconds—and the machine will be under way, smoothly, with the clutch fully home.

At this stage, it is better not to change gear, but to concentrate instead, upon controlling the speed by use of the throttle. Both the 175 and the 250 c.c. B.S.A. and Triumph machines have a quick throttle response, so it is essential that the throttle is not jerked. It should be rotated backwards smoothly to accelerate, and forwards smoothly to slow down. At the end of the road, if you do not feel up to making a sharp turn at this stage, pull out the clutch, use the neutral selector control to engage neutral, and apply the brakes to stop the machine. Then wheel it round, make another start, and repeat the exercise again and again until both throttle and clutch control are perfect.

Once this has been done, it is easy enough to make a slow turn at the end of a run. Having glanced behind to make sure the road is clear, and given the appropriate signal, the machine is leaned slightly to the right and given a little throttle to help it climb the camber. The angle of bank is held constant, unless the machine is turning too slowly, until it is facing in the opposite direction.

Before long, it will be possible to go through the gears as well on each run. To change from a lower gear to a higher gear it is necessary to make several movements almost simultaneously.

First, the throttle is snapped shut and, at the same time, the clutch is drawn out. There is no need to be gentle about this. Both movements can be as deliberate as you like—but they *must* be made in unison.

As the clutch is disengaged, the right foot is used to *snick* the gear pedal backwards to engage the next gear. Then, as the foot reaches the end of its travel, the clutch is released in a single hand movement, performed as quickly as possible, and the throttle is snapped open again. The aim is to make the entire change just as fast as the controls can be operated.

To change down, the easiest method is to pull out the clutch and almost at once, press the gear pedal forward, and "blip" the throttle to raise engine speed slightly. As the throttle hand moves, the left hand releases the clutch, and the change is made.

The object of the "blip" is to raise the engine speed momentarily to ease engagement, since, speed for speed, a lower gear means that more revolutions are needed from the engine. Later on, it will become possible to make smooth, clean changes simply by leaving the throttle open and allowing the engine to speed up to match the road speed in the lower gear. That, however, is a joy reserved for the "polishing," not the elementary, stage of riding.

Both when moving off, and when coming to a halt, the place for the feet is on the footboard. It is a bad mistake to leave the feet trailing for an instant longer than necessary, since no rider is properly balanced on the machine until his feet are up. On take-off, the feet should be raised as soon as the clutch begins to "bite," and when halting one foot should be put down only a fraction of a second before the machine comes to a standstill. The aim should be to ride to a standstill feet-up, and then to place one foot on the ground before the machine can move out of a vertical position.

More especially if their previous experience has been confined to riding a pedal cycle, most learners make the mistake of using only the rear brake and ignoring the front brake when stopping. This is exactly the opposite of what *should* be done. Of the two brakes on a scooter, the front is the more powerful, and it is less likely to provoke a skid. Skilled riders use the front brake, almost exclusively, for checking speed when manoeuvring, and they give it a "lead" over the rear brake for making a quick stop.

The reason for this is simple. When the rear brake is applied, the effect on the scooter is to transfer the weight forwards off the rear wheel. When the front brake is applied, weight transfer is still forward, and

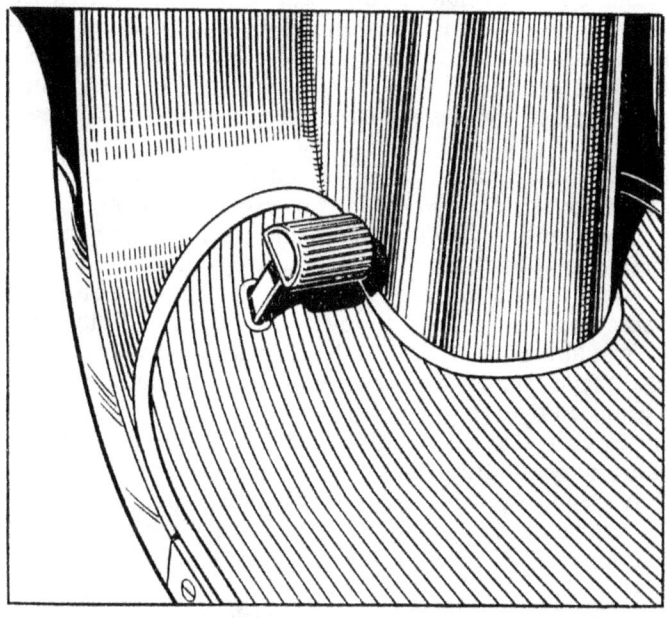

Fig. 9. The Rear Brake

The single pedal on the left-hand footboard controls the rear brake. The two brakes of the scooter are not interconnected.

this glues the front wheel to the ground, giving better tyre adhesion and better braking.

During this formative stage of riding, then, disregard the rear brake, and use the front brake alone for making all practice stops. Once you have acquired the "feel" of front wheel braking, go one stage further and, after applying the front brake, increase the braking power by a gentle application of the rear brake as well. Finally, practise using both brakes hard, while still applying the front brake a split second before the rear one.

When braking hard, the initial movement is to flick the throttle shut, and to apply little more than finger pressure to the front brake. Then as the left foot begins to apply the back brake, the finger pressure on the front brake is increased, until both brakes are hard on. As the scooter slows, withdraw the clutch. The result should be a quick, straight-line stop.

It is a mistake, of course, to use the brakes for all deceleration, and when the roads are slippery it is best to use them very sparingly indeed. Most of the time, the right amount of deceleration is obtained by use of the throttle alone, with assistance from the brakes when a fair amount of speed needs to be lost.

To slow down by use of the gearbox entails nothing more complicated than making a normal change down, but with the throttle closed again as soon as the lower gear is engaged, so that the scooter is decelerated against the resistance of the engine. Subsequent downward changes are made as soon as the road speed comes within the range of the next-lowest gear, and the brakes are used only to "kill" the last few miles per hour.

Use of the "over-run," as this is called, used to be considered the hallmark of the skilled rider. Now, however, the generally accepted style is to lose speed by applying the brakes and then selecting the appropriate gear. That saves wear on the engine and transmission.

This system is used, for example, when descending a steep hill. If the brakes were applied all the way down—as they would otherwise have to be—they would become very hot, the linings would wear, and the brakes might also "fade" under the influence of heat. Instead, the main braking force is provided by the engine, and the brakes merely have to be brought into play to keep the speed within safe limits. For this purpose, a few spasmodic and gentle front-brake "dabs" are normally sufficient, and the brakes have ample opportunity to cool between applications.

Like a bicycle, a scooter is steered by being leaned to one side or the other, but unlike a bicycle its handlebars are not perceptibly moved during turns.

When a two-wheeler—or any other vehicle, come to that—is made to turn, the previously balanced forces which were maintaining its equilibrium are upset by the arrival of another force—centrifugal force—which tends to pull it across the road away from the centre of the turn. If the turn was made with the vehicle upright, the rider would either have to let it skid outwards, or else incline his own weight to balance this upsetting force. Neither solution is a very good one; instead, the machine is leaned into the turn. This has two effects. One is to cause the front wheel to steer into the turn, owing to its castor action, and the other is to place the centre of gravity of the machine to one side. This—if the machine happened to be stationary—would make it topple over. In other words, it brings into play a second upsetting force. Thus, while centrifugal force is trying to drag the machine bodily out of the turn, this other force which the rider has induced is trying to make it fall inwards towards the centre of the turn. The obvious result is a draw! The two forces balance out, and the machine turns quite smoothly.

For each combination of radius of turn and speed there is really only one correct angle of bank, but luckily it is not necessary to go to all the complication of rate-of-turn meters and inclinometers to ensure that all is well—the rider can *feel* whether or not the scooter is turning smoothly, and can increase or decrease the angle of bank to suit the case.

Most of the work of cornering has, in fact, to be done before the corner is reached. The object is simply stated, if not so simply achieved—to arrive at the corner at the right speed, in the right gear, on the right point on the road.

As the scooter comes towards a corner, the rider has to weigh up the pattern of the road, and decide just how to tackle the turn. All braking and slowing has to be done with the machine upright, and it therefore has to be done on the "approach." The first stage is to lose speed on the over-run. Whether third, second or first gear is to be used for the actual corner depends upon the sharpness of the turn. "The sharper the turn the lower the gear" is a good rule.

The scooter is allowed to approach the corner in the gear selected, with the throttle shut, slowing against compression. If necessary, the brakes are applied. When the scooter reaches a point at which the rider can *just* see through the bend the machine is heeled over, and the throttle opened very gently to drive the machine round. It should follow a true arc, concentric with the inner curve of the corner. As the machine is straightened out, the throttle opening is increased, and the scooter is accelerated away from the corner. The exit speed should be higher than the speed at which the corner was entered.

SIDECAR DRIVING

With their powerful engines, the B.S.A. and Triumph machines are ideally suited for use with a sidecar. Driving a sidecar, however, is an art in itself, quite distinct from solo work.

One of the greatest errors made by beginners with a combination is to oversteer. Sidecar outfits have very sensitive steering, equivalent to a car in which direct gearing is employed. Thus the slightest movement of the handlebar is sufficient to set the outfit turning. If the bars are visibly deflected from the central position the resulting turn is very sharp indeed. For all normal work, the bars should not so much be turned as pressed, very gently, with the palm of the hand.

With a sidecar outfit, too, the question of stability needs to be more closely studied. No vehicle on the road has a better resistance to skidding than has a well-aligned sidecar outfit, and none can recover so quickly and effortlessly from a skid once one has developed. But no vehicle will lift a wheel as easily as a sidecar outfit which is being mishandled, and it is vital that the correct driving technique should be applied at all times.

When a sidecar outfit is turned to the left, centrifugal force tries to pull it to the right. This has the effect of placing an increased load on the scooter wheels, but of lightening the load on the sidecar wheel. If the turn is sufficiently sharp, the centrifugal force is able to overcome the weight of the sidecar completely, and the sidecar wheel lifts into the air.

On a right-hand corner, the weight transfer is from the scooter wheels on to the sidecar wheel. Once again, if the centrifugal force is great enough it can cause the rear wheel of the scooter to lift. This has the effect of pivoting the scooter about a base-line whose points of contact with the ground are the sidecar wheel and the front wheel. This baseline offers no resistance to the overturning couple which has been set up, and if the forces have got well and truly out of hand the machine simply somersaults.

This may, perhaps, sound drastic, but the fate of a solo scooter would be no better if no correcting force were applied on cornering, and the same use of correcting forces holds good with the sidecar.

On a left-hand bend, it is necessary to balance a force which is trying to upset the machine to the right. This is provided, quite simply, by accelerating—an action which brings into play a new set of forces which hold the sidecar wheel firmly on the ground.

Where the turn is to the right, centrifugal force is acting in the opposite direction, and so the opposite course is adopted. The machine is braked slightly. This slows the scooter, but not the unbraked wheel of the sidecar, so the effect is the same as if there had been acceleration on the sidecar wheel and constant speed on the scooter wheels. Once again, the forces are in equilibrium, and the outfit turns smoothly.

When cornering with a sidecar outfit, then, it is essential not to approach left-hand bends without some reserve of power in hand to enable the machine to be accelerated, and the gear selected for the bend must have a range sufficient to enable acceleration to be maintained all the way round. On right-hand bends, it helps to drop into a lower gear, as well as braking slightly, to set up the maximum turning moment and ease the effect of the adverse camber of the bend.

Another peculiarity of the sidecar outfit is apparent when braking. If the brakes were applied hard, with the machine travelling straight ahead, it would tend to broadside violently to the right. This, of course, is a result of the entire braking effort being concentrated on one side. The scooter wheels slow down, but the sidecar wheel is unbraked, and continues at the same speed as before. It therefore tries to turn the outfit around the decelerating scooter. Again, the technique is quite simple. As the brakes are applied, gentle hand pressure is placed on the handlebars to give them a slight bias to the left. The result is that the machine travels in a straight line. In an emergency, however, the machine's inherent swing to the right, if no steering correction is applied, can sometimes be turned to advantage, as, for example, when violent avoiding action is needed.

On slippery roads, the sidecar outfit comes into its own, and the outrigged, free-rolling sidecar wheel becomes a valuable ally. If a skid tries to develop, it must of necessity push the sidecar wheel off course. But the wheel resists this, and automatically pushes the outfit back to its original position. Under these conditions, the sidecar wheel does, in fact, anticipate skids, and corrects them almost before they can start.

It is essential, however, that any sidecar fitted to a scooter should be properly aligned. A well-set-up sidecar will need next to no effort to steer, and on a level road with no camber will tend to run straight without any noticeable pressure being needed on the bars. On a heavily-cambered road, only a very slight pressure with the left hand should be necessary to hold a straight course.

If an outfit is hard to steer it is undoubtedly misaligned, and adjustments to the settings should be made to bring them within the limits prescribed by the manufacturers. Even if it is not dangerous, a badly aligned sidecar outfit is tiring to drive.

CHAPTER IV

FAULT TRACING

WHEN a doctor wishes to diagnose a patient's illness, he works methodically, listing the various symptoms to build up an overall picture of the complaint. This done, he can identify it, and give treatment accordingly. Exactly the same type of diagnosis has to be made in the case of a scooter engine which refuses to work. Obviously, there is a fault—some *reason* why it will not work—and before the fault can be cured it has got to be located and identified. The search for it must be just as methodical as the doctor's approach.

If certain requirements are being properly fulfilled, then the engine *must* work. If it is not working, then it follows that one or more of these requirements is not being met, and fault tracing boils down to discovering which it is.

An engine *must* work if the correct charge of petrol/air mixture is being induced into the cylinder at the right time; properly compressed; fired at the right moment; and the residue properly exhausted.

The first stage in checking must, therefore, be the obvious one of ensuring that there is, in fact, a supply of petrol, and that this is reaching the carburettor.

As an invariable first step, always look into the fuel tank to make sure that it contains sufficient fuel. Then, operate the fuel tap to make certain that it is turned on and, if the fuel level in the tank is low, make sure that the tap is switched over to the reserve position.

Next on the list comes the task of ascertaining that the fuel is reaching the carburettor. Flowing of the fuel could be prevented by a blockage in the tap; a blockage in the pipe; an air lock; a choked filter on the float chamber; or a jammed needle valve.

Where the carburettor is fitted with a "tickler," it is often sufficient merely to depress this for a matter of five seconds, and check that the float chamber floods. If it does, petrol will drip from the carburettor. Where this method is inappropriate, the chamber can be opened up for inspection. First, however, switch the petrol off. When the chamber is open, the fuel may be switched on again so that you can see whether or not the fuel is flowing through the needle valve properly. Look, also, for signs of dirt in the chamber itself. If there is sediment on the bottom, take the opportunity of swilling the chamber out thoroughly before everything is replaced.

Normally, this initial check on the fuel system will have taken only a matter of a few seconds to carry out. It will have given one of two answers—either that fuel is reaching the float chamber, or that it is not. If it is not, then you have found at least a contributory factor to the breakdown, and this should be rectified before proceeding.

Once again, rectification depends primarily upon isolating the exact source of the trouble, and in this case it is best to work backwards from the carburettor towards the tank.

Switch off the petrol, and undo the nut of the union connecting the fuel lead to the carburettor. Then switch on the fuel again, and check that it is flowing through the pipe. There should be quite a strong stream of fuel—not just a trickle—and if this strong flow is present, the fault obviously lies either in the filter or the valve assembly on the carburettor itself. Clean both assemblies, refit the fuel line, and try starting the engine.

Suppose, however, that *no* fuel has flowed through the pipe. That would show that the trouble lies somewhere between the free end of the pipe and the fuel tank—in the pipe itself; in the tap; or in the tank orifice. In this case, the next step will obviously be to detach the pipe, and then to switch the fuel on. If it then flowed through the tap, the pipe would be isolated as the seat of the trouble. If not, then the obvious inference would be that the tap itself was blocked with dirt, and it would have to be removed for cleaning.

It is possible for the fuel system to be at fault by supplying too much fuel, as well as by supplying too little. Overflooding, as this form of trouble is called, is easily recognizable, for fuel drips from the carburettor whenever the petrol is switched on, and the engine—if it runs at all—constantly misfires and sounds distinctly "lumpy."

Only the float assembly can be responsible for this particular form of trouble. The float may have punctured, in which case it simply sinks to the bottom of the chamber and allows the valve to remain open. More likely, however, is the ingress of dirt into the valve assembly. Even a tiny speck of hard matter is sufficient to prevent that needle seating properly, and this keeps the valve partially open. The effects of this milder form of overflooding would be more noticeable at low engine speeds, where the excess fuel was not being used up quickly enough, than at high engine speeds. Finally, the needle itself may have become bent. In each case, thorough inspection of the float assembly is the only way of pinpointing the exact cause.

Where the initial inspection of the fuel system shows no immediately obvious fault, the next stage of the fault tracing should be switched to the ignition system—always a strong suspect, especially with two-strokes. First of all, remove the sparking plug, and examine the spark gap. Obviously, it should be clear, but with two-stroke engines a condition known as "whiskering" tends to occur. Under the influence of heat, metallic particles contained in the fuel tend to weld themselves to the plug electrodes, and eventually they bridge the gap completely. When this happens, of course, no spark occurs, since the high-tension current can follow this easier path to earth.

A "whisker" is cleared by simply flicking it away with the blade of a penknife, the edge of a feeler gauge, or even with a piece of thick paper. It is best to give the plug a quick clean with a wire brush, and to re-gap it, before replacing it. Persistent "whiskering" is a sign that something else is wrong, too. It can mean that the wrong grade of plug is being used—

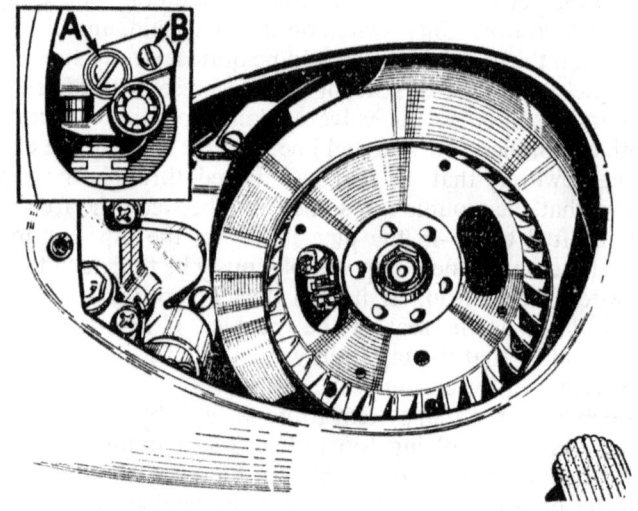

FIG. 10. THE CONTACT-BREAKER POINTS ON THE 175 C.C. MODEL
These are located inside the flywheel and are reached through the flywheel slots after removing a grille and a cover plate. To adjust the points (inset) loosen screw A and turn the eccentric screw B to vary the gap.

each engine has certain recommended grades of plug, and these recommendations should be adhered to—or that the unit is running too hot, which in turn points to bad scavenging or to a mixture which is too weak.

Where inspection of the plug shows that the spark gap is clear, and neither too closely nor too widely set, the plug should be reconnected to the H.T. lead, and then the metal body of the plug must be placed in contact with the cylinder head or some convenient metal part of the machine in such a position that the spark gap can easily be seen.

With the ignition switched on, the engine is turned over by means of the kick starter. As this is done, a good, fat spark should jump across the plug points. This check should be repeated several times, and if no spark results a brand-new plug—an essential "spare," which should always be carried—should be substituted and the check repeated. If the new plug sparks and the old one didn't, then the obvious inference is that the old plug's insulation has broken down, and fitting the new plug in its place should cure the trouble. If, on the other hand, the new plug fails as well, then the trouble lies somewhere between the spark plug terminal and the generator, and a much more exhaustive check is needed.

If, with the twin-cylinder machine, there has been a complete ignition failure, and the engine will run neither on normal nor emergency ignition, it is better to refer the whole job to a garage for checking with instruments. The likelihood is that a major failure has occurred, since the system is almost fully duplicated for each cylinder, and the odds against a simple fault causing both systems to cease operation simultaneously are astronomic.

Where one cylinder still fires, and the plug in the faulty cylinder has been exonerated, the next step is to check the two low-tension leads from the generator to the high-tension coil concerned. These leads should be securely fitted to the coil terminals, and there should be no obvious fractures. Detach the h.t. lead, and examine it carefully for any signs of breakage, or for cuts or cracks which might cause a short-circuit. On the twins, the dualseat hinge can, on occasion, trap the left-hand lead and cause sufficient damage to short out the plug.

As a double check, the h.t. lead on the other cylinder, which is known to be in order, can be detached, and fitted to the other coil. The machine is then kicked over. If it runs, the fault is pin-pointed in the ignition lead or the terminal, and re-inspection should give the exact answer.

It is possible to carry this type of check one stage further by ringing the changes not only on the ignition lead, but on the complete coil. Where a coil proves to be at fault there is, unfortunately, no alternative but to replace it, since the inference is that the internal winding has broken.

Once the high-tension side of the ignition system has been exonerated, the low-tension circuits can be checked quite easily if the engine will still run.

First, unscrew the headlamp from the front fairing, and remove from it the pilot light bulb. This should be taken out complete with its holder, and the snap-connector in the lead should be freed. This leaves about six inches of cable attached to the holder. Start the engine, and set it to tick over. The bulb holder is then pressed against the bare metal of the frame or dualseat supports while the end of the lead is placed on each low-tension terminal in turn. If current is reaching the terminal, the bulb will light. In this way, a faulty low-tension lead can be located quickly.

Should both leads to a single coil give no current flow, the inference must be either that the fault lies in the generator or contact-breaker unit. Where ignition failure is complete, it is possible that the lead from the alternator to the ignition switch has fractured.

The contact-breakers should also be examined; their settings checked (18 thou. on the 175 c.c. model, 15 thou. on the 250 c.c. model); and all connexions examined.

Complete engine failure for any reason other than ignition or fuel trouble is unlikely, save in the somewhat remote event of such a vital part as the timing gear drive to the camshaft being stripped. Other troubles are, therefore, likely to show themselves in reduced performance or erratic running.

One of the likelier causes of lack of pulling power on the twins is the tappet setting being incorrect. The tappets are given a slight clearance to enable expansion to take place without adverse affects on the valve seating. If, however, a tappet is set too tight, expansion as the engine warms up will tend to hold the valve away from its seat slightly, and thus reduce the compression in that particular cylinder.

It is possible, where this is suspected, to deduce where the fault lies from the way in which the engine behaves. If the inlet valve is not being properly closed, there will be a tendency for the engine to "spit back" through the carburettor, since some mixture will be driven back during the compression stroke. Where the exhaust valve is not seating properly, the mixture tends to be driven into the exhaust system, and to be ignited there by the heat, giving a constant banging or rumbling in the exhaust pipe.

In both cases, the affected cylinder tends to run hot, and this naturally aggravates the trouble by causing greater expansion, making the tappet press even more tightly on the valve than before.

A rough check can be made without removing the rocker covers by placing the machine on the stand, with the engine running, and detaching each ignition lead in turn. When the lead is taken off the cylinder which is *not* developing its full power the engine speed will fall only slightly. When the lead is removed from the cylinder which *is* contributing its full power the fall in engine speed will be marked, and the unit may even stop.

It is not possible, of course, to re-set the tappets accurately when the engine is hot, but since damage to the valve seats can result from running with a tight tappet it is permissible, in an emergency, to slacken off the wrongly-set tappet until there is just a barely-perceptible amount of play. This, of course, is only a "get you home" measure, and once the engine has cooled, the tappets must be reset in the normal way.

Loss of compression can be caused in several other ways, although none of them is at all usual. Distortion of the cylinder head/barrel joint, which could result if the engine is run when suffering from chronic overheating, is one of them. This, obviously, calls for workshop treatment. In such a case, there might be a distinct hiss of escaping gas audible at the joint all the time the engine was running, and since air would be induced into the cylinder, thus diluting the mixture, the engine would also tend to overheat. A leakage of oil from the broken joint might also be noticeable.

Following a seizure of the engine—either through working it too hard before it was run in, or from failure of the lubrication system—piston rings might be fractured. Besides losing compression, the engine would also begin to take oil into the combustion chamber. This oil, of course, would burn, and the resulting smoke would issue from the exhaust pipe.

Where an engine, after a seizure, loses power and smokes, the only wise course is to stop immediately, since the rings are almost certainly broken.

FAULT TRACING

Any further running might easily cause deep score marks on the bores—where the broken ends of the rings would act as efficient cutting tools—and the engine might then be virtually ruined.

Exactly the same process of elimination is employed when tracing faults in the lighting system. Faced with electricity, of course, most laymen simply give it best first time, but in actual fact electrical work is reasonably straightforward providing that one magic word "circuit" is borne in mind.

Circuits are, in fact, the key to electricity. If electricity is present and the circuit is complete, then the current *must* flow through it. If electricity is present but is not flowing, then it follows that the circuit is not complete.

Faulty circuits are of two types—the open circuit and the short circuit. In the first case, there is a break in the circuit, and the wires on the far side of the break, viewed from the electrical source, are "dead." In the second case, the current is still flowing but is following a shorter path to earth—as would be the case, for example, if one end of a "live" lead had become detached from its terminal and had earthed itself on a frame tube.

Obviously, the first essential is to be able to understand a wiring diagram. At first sight, this may appear disconcertingly like a plan of a rather complicated suburban railway—and, oddly enough, it is not at all a bad idea to regard it in this light. If the various leads are thought of as railway tracks, and the current as a train which has to pass along the tracks, the whole idea becomes enormously simplified. It is as well to remember, however, that one important main line is not shown. This is the earth return. One terminal of the battery is connected straight to earth, and all the components are similarly earthed. This, therefore, forms one complete half of the circuit.

To trace, for example, the circuit which lights the main headlamp bulb filament, one takes as the starting point the unearthed terminal of the battery, and follows the lead shown on the wiring diagram leading from this terminal. It goes to a point on the lighting switch. From the switch, another lead is taken, through the dip switch, to the headlamp bulb, and thence to earth. If, therefore, the tumbler of the lighting switch connects these two main switch terminals there will be a complete circuit. It will run from the positive terminal of the battery to terminal 10 of the lighting switch; through the switch tumbler to terminal 3 of the switch; from terminal 3 to the dip switch, and from the dip switch to either the main filament or the dip filament of the bulb, depending upon the dip switch setting. After passing through the filament it returns to earth, and since the positive terminal of the battery is also connected to earth there is a complete circuit. Sometimes, where a rather more complicated circuit is involved, it helps to trace it out individually on a sheet of paper.

Having found the circuit, the next job is to check it. Obviously, the first stage is to find out whether or not electricity is present and here, again, the pilot bulb, its holder and its lead can be pressed into service. Detach

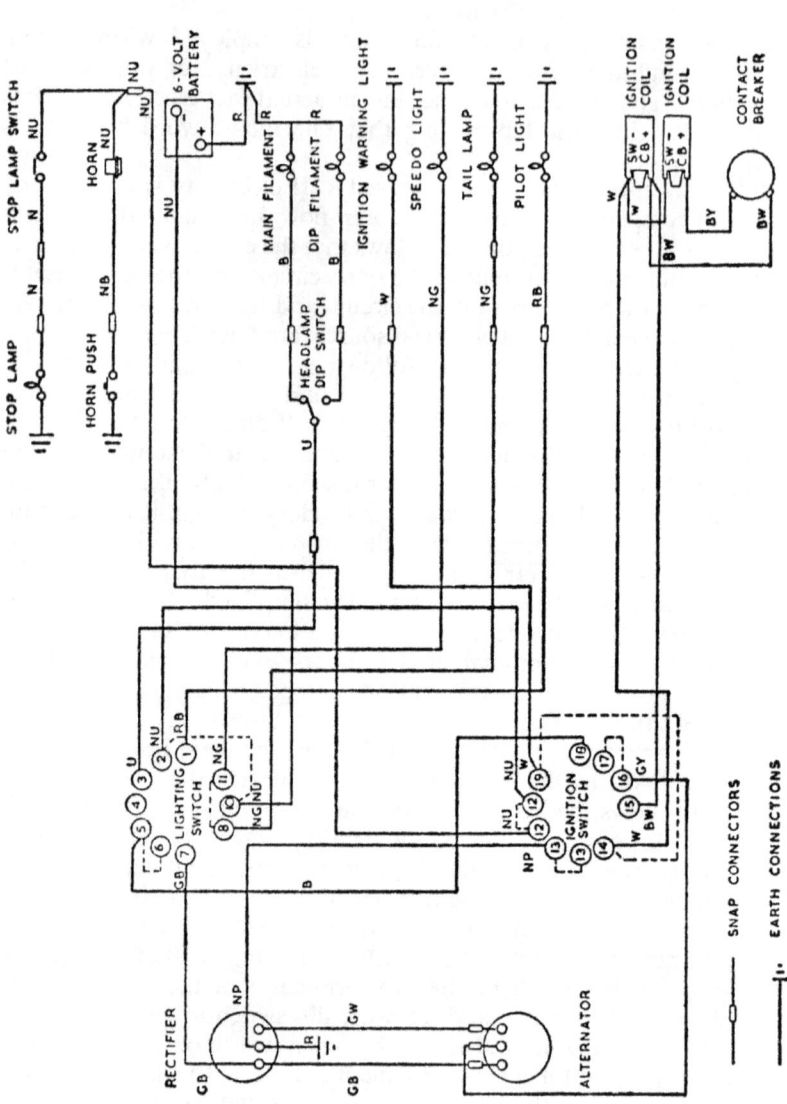

Fig. 11. The Wiring of the Kick-starter Version of the 250 c.c. Scooter

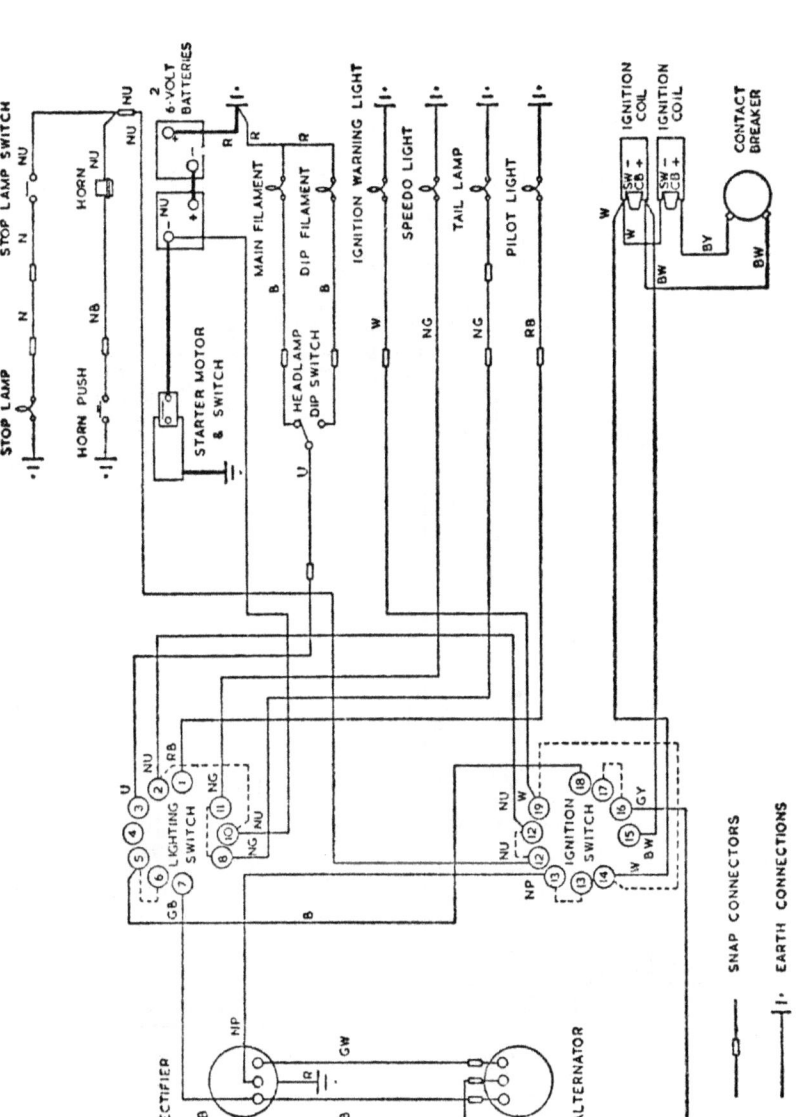

Fig. 12. Wiring Diagram for the 250 c.c. Self-Starter Machine

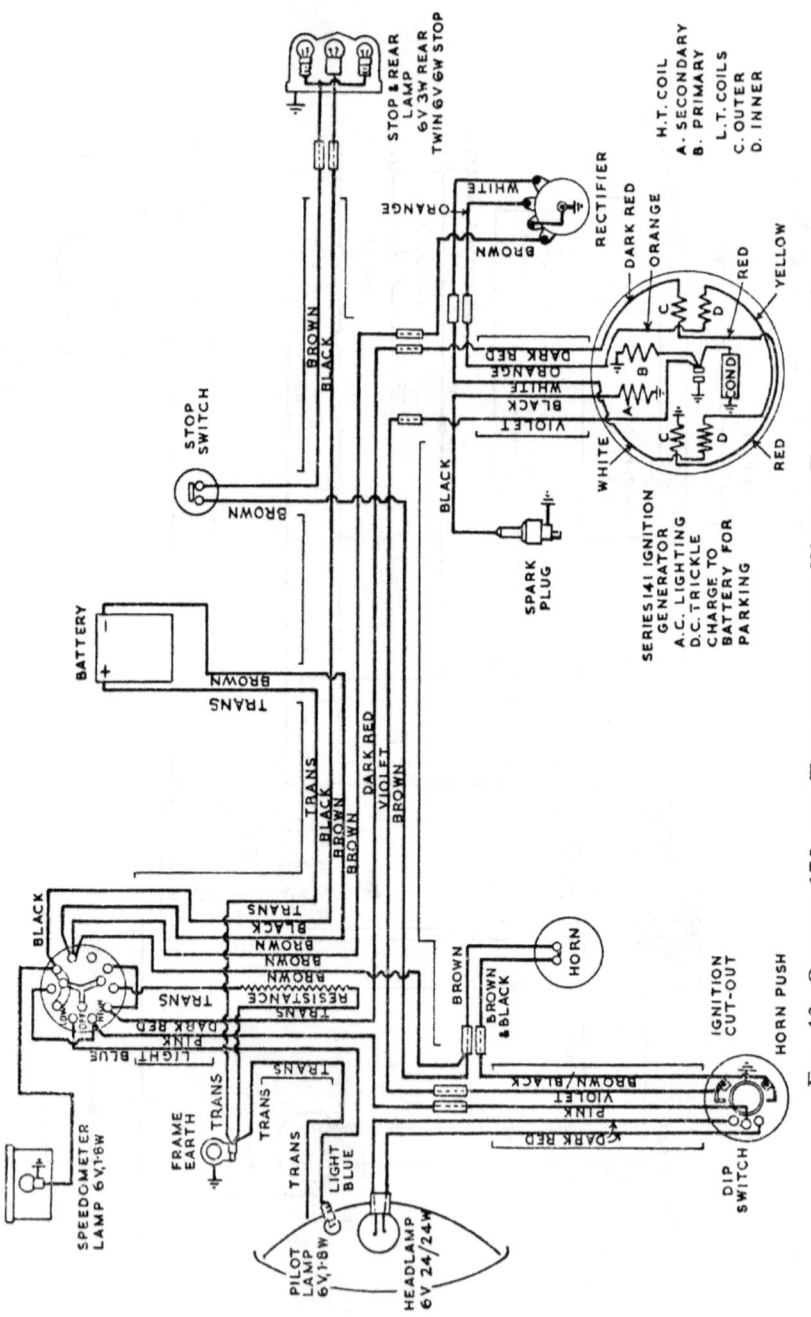

Fig. 13. On the 175 c.c. Two-stroke, the Wiring Follows this Layout

them from the headlamp, open the battery box, and connect the bulb across the battery terminals. If the battery is in order the lamp will light.

Once certain on this point, it becomes necessary to check each individual lead in the circuit in question. This is made considerably easier by the fact that each wire is given an outer casing of a different colour.

In the circuit used here as an example, the next step would be to lift out the lighting switch, complete with its leads, and to apply the lamp lead to the correct terminal, while earthing the holder. Once again, the lamp should light, indicating that electricity was flowing as far as the terminal. The switch should then be set to the appropriate position, and the check repeated on the second terminal. If that passes muster, the next stage of the wiring—from the light switch to the dip switch, should be similarly checked. Finally, the one remaining lead—from the dip switch to the headlamp bulb, would be tested. This assumes, naturally enough, that one has had the "savvy" to examine the headlamp bulb first, to make sure that the filament is intact!

When the faulty section of wiring is located, it should be closely examined so that the exact cause of failure can be ascertained. A short circuit can often be detected by shaking the wire and listening carefully. As it contacts metal, the characteristic crackling of current short-circuiting can easily be heard. A break in the wire, concealed by the outer insulation, can usually be found by holding each end and pulling gently. If the inner cable has broken, the lead will stretch at the point at which the fracture has occurred.

Where the suspect lead is a very long one, and is inaccessible, an alternative method of checking is to by-pass it with a temporary external lead. This is connected to the terminal at each end, and the switch is then operated. If the hitherto inoperative component—a tail light, for instance—works when thus connected, it shows that the fault is in the lead. In some cases, it is possible to draw a new lead through a conduit by using the old lead as a guide. The new lead is securely fastened to the old one—by wiring the terminals together, for example, and the old lead is then withdrawn, pulling the new lead into position.

When repairing fractured leads, it is important to ensure that no undue electrical stresses are set up, and that the insulation is made good. All joints should be twisted together as neatly as possible, and well wound with insulating tape to make leakage impossible. Where terminals have been undone, they must be done up again tightly, since a loose terminal can cause electrical stresses through spasmodic breaking of the circuit. Where a soldered joint has failed, it is essential that it be remade with solder, and not merely taped.

With these pointers borne in mind, there is no reason why the scooter owner should not be able to trace most faults occurring in the engine and the electrical systems of his machine, and provide at least a temporary cure for them.

CHAPTER V

THE TOOL KIT

It is virtually impossible to make a bigger mistake, when setting out to maintain or overhaul a scooter, than attempting to do the job with inadequate tools. To carry out even routine maintenance jobs properly calls for the use of a good-quality tool kit, while major overhauls can quite often require the use of special tools, designed by the manufacturer to do one specific job and one only.

Each B.S.A. or Triumph scooter is equipped with a tool kit upon delivery, but with the exception of one or two items this is intended to act only as a stand-by kit, capable of dealing with road-side emergencies, but very definitely not suited to the sterner work of, say, completely stripping the engine—or even of decarbonizing.

In addition, the use of special service tools for such jobs as removing the flywheel or the clutch centre, or for parting the flywheels of the 175 c.c. unit, is not dictated simply by lack of intelligence on the part of the designer, nor because the makers can sell such tools at a profit. It is dictated by the very fact that these scooters are made to precision-engineering standards, and that some of the assembly work is such that only special tools have the slightest chance of freeing the various components concerned.

Even where the jobs to be tackled do not call for the use of special tools, they will still require the use of *good* tools. Cheap tools are a bad investment, for not only do they not wear as well as they should, but they also have an infuriating habit of ruining nuts and bolts.

The first essential is to buy a really good set of chrome-vanadium open-ended spanners in Whitworth sizes. A set of half a dozen double-ended spanners will give a range of sizes sufficient for most of the work, and will cost only a couple of pounds.

Next, it is essential to have a set of strong box spanners or, even better, a set of socket spanners. Ring spanners are more of a luxury—they are less handy in confined spaces than are open-enders or sockets—although they do enable a very good grip to be obtained.

Almost equally essential are a pair of really good screwdrivers, with insulated handles. One screwdriver with a $\frac{3}{16}$ in. blade and an electrical screwdriver with a $\frac{1}{8}$ in. blade are the minimum requirements.

You will also need a pair of pliers equipped with wire-cutters. Pliers are indispensable for electrical and cable work. A nest of small B.A. spanners is also useful for electrical work.

USING YOUR TOOLS

There is really rather more to using even the simplest hand tools than merely placing them in position and tugging hard. Each particular type of spanner has its own characteristics, and each is better suited for one particular type of job.

The great all-rounders are unquestionably the open-enders. These can be used in confined spaces, and they have the great advantage that the jaws are angled. This means that an open-ender can be used to loosen an awkwardly situated nut and then, when the limit of its movement has been reached, reversed to give fresh purchase. In this way, it is possible to undo a recalcitrant nut by easy stages.

It is, of course, essential that only the right size of spanner should be used. The open-ended spanner is designed to apply its pressure on the flats of a nut or bolt, and it is consequently made with jaws of just the right width to grip its bolt. If a larger spanner is used the jaws will press against the angles of the bolt, instead of gripping the flats. One of two things can happen here. Either the spanner gouges away the angle of the bolt, giving a rounded head which no ordinary spanner could grip thereafter, or else the bolt head slightly springs the jaws of the spanner, which is promptly ruined.

Damage to the jaws can also be caused by applying excessive force when trying to free a bolt which refuses to budge. There is a temptation, under these circumstances, to slip a piece of piping over the free end of the spanner to increase the leverage. Although this *is* permissible where due care is used, it is all too easy to apply excessive force and to spring the jaws of the spanner.

Ring, box or socket spanners are at a great advantage when really obstinate nuts have to be dealt with. Ring and socket spanners both grip on the angles, not on the flats. They are, consequently, able to apply pressure at half a dozen points, where the open-ended spanner can do so only at two. Box spanners, providing they are stoutly constructed, go one stage better. A box spanner applies force at both angles and flats, all the way round the bolt. Frequently, however, the tommy bar used to turn the box spanner simply bends under the strain, or else the amount of offset between the part of the spanner holding the bolt and the tommy bar hole where the pressure is applied tilts the spanner, which then rides off the hexagon.

When using a spanner to tighten nuts or bolts, it is important to remember that too much force should not be used. Spanners are made long enough to ensure that, for any given size of bolt, mere hand pressure applied through the full leverage of the spanner will tighten the bolt adequately. If excessive force is used the actual material of the bolt can be weakened sufficiently to cause it to fracture.

This point should also be borne in mind when tightening bolts which are threaded into light alloy. Here, the steel bolt is much harder than the material into which it is screwed, and over-enthusiasm with the spanner can easily strip the thread inside the hole.

Pliers, of course, should never be used as a makeshift spanner, since the jaws can never be parallel, and the serrated pipe grip is almost perilously liable to slip. A rounded hexagon is the inevitable result if it does.

Adjustable spanners should never be allowed near the machine! These are a butcher's tool—not a mechanic's. Here again, it is impossible to align the jaws with sufficient accuracy to enable a satisfactory grip to be obtained.

Screwdrivers should have their blades properly ground so that, in side view, the blade is at first concave, and then runs parallel to the tip. This enables the blade to seat itself properly in the slot, and to apply pressure which is evenly distributed. A screwdriver whose blade, in side view, is wedge-shaped does not seat properly, and instead of an even pressure on the sides of the slot it exerts all its force on the edges which, understandably, tend to crumble under the strain.

After use, all tools should be wiped clean. They should be kept in a dry place, protected from dust by being wrapped in rag, and if they are used fairly infrequently they should also be very lightly oiled, the light film of lubricant, of course, being wiped off before they are again put to use.

CHAPTER VI

THE CYCLE PARTS

GENERALLY speaking, the cycle parts of a scooter are the frame, forks, wheels and brakes, but the bodywork, too, can be considered as falling within this category. On both B.S.A. and Triumph 175 c.c. and 250 c.c. scooters, the actual design of these components is identical, the only difference being in the finish applied, and in the obviously necessary use of modified designs of certain minor components in the smaller-engined machine. These include a somewhat different instrument panel; engine mounting bracket; starter pedal; and a few other ancillary units. There are, also, a few differences between kick-starter and self-starter equipped models.

Thanks to its sturdy construction and basically simple design, the frame and fork assembly of the B.S.A./Triumph scooters makes little demand upon its owner's time, and since generous bearing areas are used, and positive lubrication applied to the vital swinging-arm bearing, these machines should be able to cover considerable mileages before any major work need be done.

The handling and safety of the scooters, however, depends upon the correct alignment and steering geometry being maintained, and if a machine is involved in an accident it is wise to check that the frame has not been distorted as a result. This is fairly simply done. The vertical alignment of the wheels can be checked visually, merely by placing the machine on its stand, propping the handlebars so that they are properly centred, and sighting along the centre line of the machine, from the front, from a distance of some ten yards. Both wheels should be in line with the axis of the steering head.

Misalignment due to twisting—possible if the machine has fallen heavily—can be located by placing a suitable, straight-edged length of board in contact with the wheels, and raised some three inches from the ground. This board should touch each tyre in two places. If any serious deviation from the true alignment is found the job is one for the factory, who have the necessary jigs for resetting the frame tubes. Such work should never, of course, be attempted by the private owner, since errors of as little as a single degree can have deleterious effects on the machine's handling.

Barring accidents, the only work which is necessary on the frame is to give the steering head bearing adjustment a periodic check. With use, the bearing balls and races which form the head bearings tend to settle down and to wear. If this is left uncorrected, the fork assembly becomes free to move backwards and forwards slightly, and some of the accuracy of the steering is lost. In addition, heavy loads are placed on slack bearings under acceleration or braking conditions, and damage to the races may result.

The adjustment of the bearings is correct when, with the brake applied, no movement between fork bridge and head is felt at the lower end of the steering head when the machine is rocked backwards and forwards. A

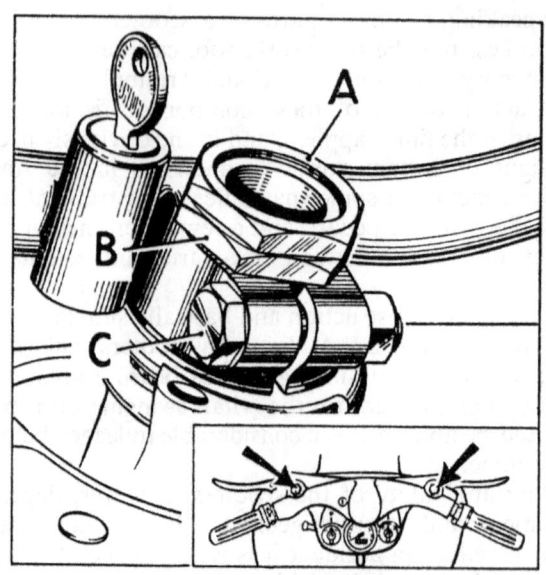

FIG. 14. HOW TO REACH THE STEERING HEAD ADJUSTMENT (INSET)
Remove the two Phillips-headed screws (arrowed) which secure the fairing. When the pinch-bolt C has been loosened, slacken lock nut A and take up play by means of nut B.

the same time, the fork should turn freely from lock to lock, with no suggestion of a tight spot.

The adjustment for the head bearings is concealed beneath the pressed-steel handlebar fairing. This is removed by slipping one hand beneath each of the two holding-down bolts to prevent the nut turning, and loosening the Phillips-headed screw with the special screwdriver provided in the toolkit. This done, the fairing can be lifted off.

The pinch-bolt on the handlebar clip must then be slackened, and the uppermost of the two large nuts on the fork stem loosened. This is the lock nut, whose purpose is to prevent the lower nut from turning accidentally.

Next, the lower nut must be turned slowly to the right to tighten it down. Very little movement is required—say an eighth of a turn at a time—and between movements the adjustment should be checked by rocking the fork backwards and forwards and by swinging the bars from lock to lock. It is important to remember that if the bearing is overtightened the forks will be unable to steer the machine properly, and the scooter will then tend to "run out" on corners.

When the correct adjustment has been reached, the lower nut is held securely with a spanner, and the top nut is tightened so that it locks down hard on the lower nut. The pinch bolt is then retightened, and the fairing replaced.

Fork Removal and Replacement. To remove the front fork completely—to renew a suspect bearing, for example—the handlebar fairing must be removed, and the clutch and brake cables disconnected from the levers. There is a simple method of doing this. Pull the lever as far as it will go, and while holding it there take a firm grip on the outer casing of the cable. Then, moving both hands in unison, slowly release the lever, and pull the outer casing away from the bar. As soon as the nipple clears its housing, swing the casing forwards and release it. The inner wire can then be slipped out of the lever.

The front brake cable must next be disconnected from the brake arm. Pull out the split pin which locates the clevis pin; pull the clevis pin out of its hole in the brake arm; and unscrew the brake cable adjuster from the light-alloy sliding member of the fork. Next, slacken the two screws which clamp the twist-grip to the handlebars, and the two small screws securing the dip switch. Finally, loosen the pinch bolt on the handlebar clip.

To remove the fork the front of the scooter will have to be blocked up to give at least six inches clearance between the ground and the tyre, and since this will remove the scooter's weight from the front wheel it is best to loosen the wheel nuts at this stage. That done, lift the front end on to the blocks, and then complete the removal of the wheel.

The two large nuts on the stem are next on the list. These are removed completely, and the handlebar assembly can then be lifted off. After this, the handlebar steering lock plate is removed—make a careful note, first, of its exact position so that it can be replaced correctly—and after this the dust cover and the long metal "key" can be taken from the stem. It will probably be necessary to prise out the key, which is a tight fit in its slot, and care must be taken not to damage either the key itself or the surfaces of the slot.

A large piece of clean rag should now be slipped under the fork bridge and held there as the fork is pulled gently down, so that any bearing balls which fall are caught. These will come from the lower race, which contains 28 balls. These should be collected, and placed in a tin. The similar number of balls from the top race should be placed in a separate container, since it is inadvisable to mix the two sets.

To refit the forks, grease is applied to the two cups on the frame, and the 28 lower balls are positioned in the lower one. The rubber dust excluder, if this has been removed, should be slipped into place on the head, and pushed up sufficiently high to avoid any interference with the fitting operation.

The fork stem is then pushed into the steering head, and held in place while the bearing balls are placed in the top bearing cup. The top cone is

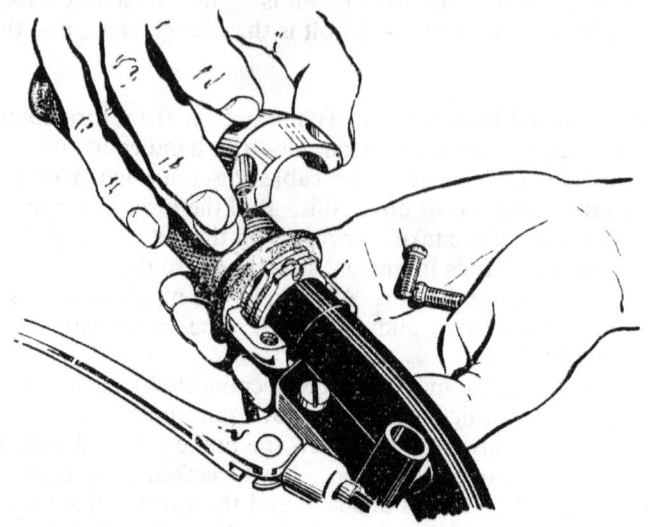

FIG. 15. THE TWIST-GRIP CASING

The two halves are secured by screws. Inside the casing, the control cable and nipple should seat properly in the drum, and should be kept well greased.

replaced, followed by the dust cover, and the long key. This done, the handlebar lock plate and handlebar clip is placed over the stem, carefully guiding the clip so that the key engages with the slot. The two large nuts are then replaced, and the bearings adjusted. The pinch bolt is then tightened; the twist-grip reclamped; the dip switch screwed down; controls reconnected; and the handlebar fairing replaced.

Removing and Refitting Brake Shoes. Ample adjustment is provided for both front and rear brakes, and it should be quite unnecessary to remove the shoes for many thousands of miles. When all the adjustment has been taken up, however, the existing shoes will have to be replaced with service shoes. These are used shoes to which new linings have been fitted. While it *is* possible to economize by fitting new linings to the existing shoes, it is really a job which is best left to the experts, since the efficiency of the brakes depends upon the security of the rivets used to hold the linings to the shoes.

To reach the front brake shoes, it is first necessary to remove the wheel.

The cap fitted in the end of the wheel hub must then be screwed out. This has a left-hand thread, so that it must be turned clockwise to loosen and anti-clockwise to tighten. You will probably find that the whole hub tends to turn, and to prevent this the brake must be applied while the initial pressure is brought to bear on the cap.

Beneath the cap is the spindle nut, which is held by a tab washer. The tab must be flattened out, using a drift and a hammer, and the nut can

FIG. 16. REMOVAL OF THE FRONT BRAKE SHOES
This calls for the use of a special extractor to draw the brake drum off the spindle.

then be unscrewed. This has a normal right-handed thread. The brake drum, together with the wheel bearings, is now free, but they may need to be drawn off the spindle with a special extractor (Tool No. 61-5033) since the bearings are a press fit on both spindle and drum.

The brake shoes are now completely exposed, and can be removed by prising them away from the brake cam at one end and from the fulcrum pin at the other.

When fitting the replacement shoes, they should first be joined together with the springs, in such a way that when they are in position the two narrow portions of the shoes will be against the brake back-plate, and not against the drum.

Pressing against the pressure of the springs, open the shoes to form a rough Vee, and fit one end over the pivot pin. Then bring the other end into position over the brake cam. Check that they are seating properly, and operate the brake once or twice to make doubly sure.

Before the drum can be refitted, the cable adjuster will need to be fully slackened, since the setting was made for worn linings, and with the thicker unused linings this setting would make it impossible to re-assemble the parts.

This done, the brake drum is eased on to the spindle and pressed lightly home. A new tab washer is then placed on the spindle, and the spindle nut is tightened. Then the tab washer is peened over to lock the nut, and the end cap refitted. Finally, the brake adjuster is used to take up any

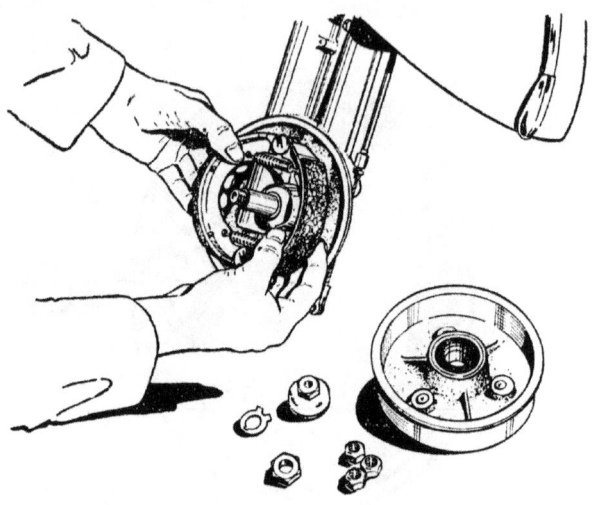

FIG. 17. WHEN THE DRUM HAS BEEN REMOVED THE BRAKE-SHOES ARE LIFTED FROM THE BACK PLATE

excessive play in the cable, and the wheel is revolved by hand to ensure that the brake is completely free.

A rather different method is used for the rear shoes. First, the rear end of the machine is placed on blocks so that the rear wheel is clear of the ground, and the three nuts holding the wheel are removed. The wheel disc is lifted off, and a screwdriver used to free the single countersunk screw which holds the brake drum to the stub axle. If this should be tight, a few gentle taps with a hammer on the screwdriver handle will loosen it.

Remove the drum, and then use a screwdriver in order to unhook the brake springs from between the shoes, which are then themselves removed.

Place the topmost replacement shoe into position, and hook into the hole nearest the brake cam one of the springs, taking care that it is fitted the same way round as in the original assembly.

A strong piece of cord is now needed. A loop, about one inch in diameter, is made in this, and the lower hook of the spring is placed in the loop. The lower shoe is held in place, and a screwdriver is used in the other end of the loop to pull the spring down to engage in its hole in the bottom shoe.

The second spring is then hooked into the hole, in the bottom shoe, nearest to the fulcrum pin. This time, the loose end is uppermost, and the

FIG. 18. REMOVAL OF THE HANDLEBAR
First take off the fairing, slacken the pinch bolt behind the clip and then remove the two large nuts on the steering head.

cord loop and screwdriver are used to pull the spring upwards to engage in the top shoe.

Once again, check the seating and operation of the shoes; slacken the adjuster; and replace the brake drum. Then refit the wheel and re-adjust the brake by racking out the cable adjuster in the normal way.

Dismantling the Front Fork. Normally, it is quite unnecessary to strip the front forks, but where this operation has to be carried out—to renew a damaged member, or to replace a spring, for instance—the first part of the work is to remove the fork from the machine, in the manner described earlier in this Chapter.

That done, the front brake is removed—again, as described earlier—but before any further work is done the entire unit must be thoroughly cleaned. First, brush it with grease solvent, and wash off all dirt with water. Then dry the fork.

To remove the sliding lower member, the two domed nuts at the bottom of the legs must be undone. In the case of the front nut, the damper rod

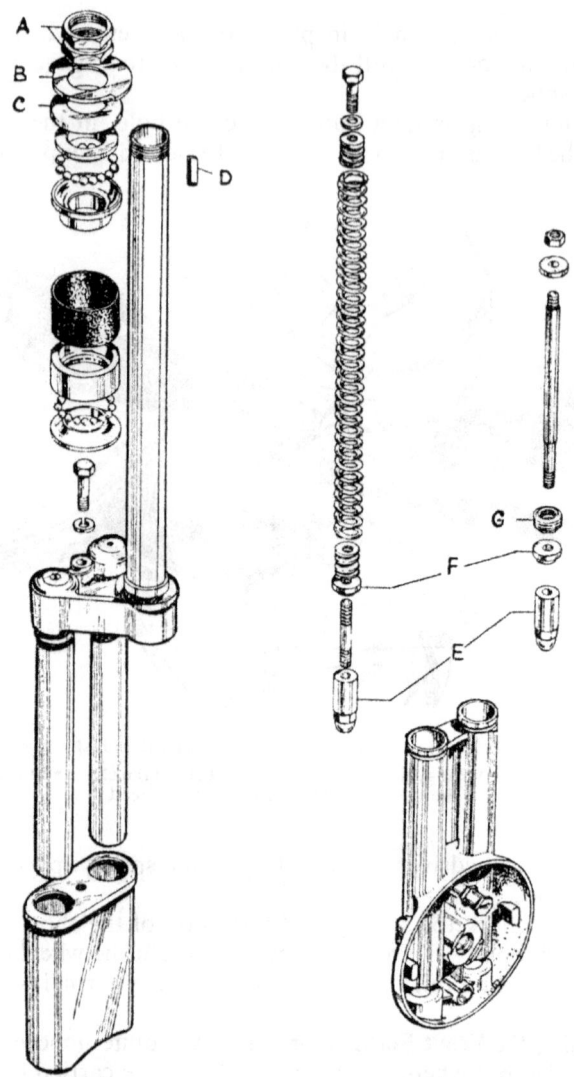

Fig. 19. The Unique Front Fork used on the B.S.A. Triumph Machines

The two large nuts A are used for adjusting and locking the steering head bearings, which are protected by dust-cap C. It is important that the Woodruff key D is accurately located if the forks are stripped. Both the spring and the damper unit have washers F, which may stick in the fork tubes when the fork is dismantled. The damper disc valve G is screwed into the front fork tube. Both damper and spring are locked to the lower sliding member by domed nuts E.

extends slightly beneath the nut, and is equipped with a slot for a screwdriver. This enables the rod to be held firm while the nut is loosened. The rear nut has no projecting rod, and is simply undone with a spanner.

A sharp pull will suffice to slide the lower member off the fork legs. Check whether or not the shouldered washers mounted on the lower ends of the spring and the damper rod have come away with the member. If so, they should be tapped out and stored away.

The spring is anchored to the fork crown by a single bolt. When this is unscrewed, the spring and its fixing scrolls are free. The damper, which is located in the front member, can be removed by unscrewing the disc valve from the bottom of the tube, and the dust cover by undoing the single bolt which holds it to the fork crown.

Fitted to the lower sliding member are the brake cam and the spindle. To remove the cam, take off the nut and washer which hold the brake arm, and slide the arm off the spindle. The cam and spindle can then be pressed out of their bearings. No attempt should be made, however, to remove the brake fulcrum pin, since this is a press fit in the member.

An interference fit is used for the spindle. First, the tab washer which locks the spindle nut, on the outer face of the sliding member, must be flattened. The nut is then removed, and the member is gently heated by immersing it in hot water for approximately one minute. No attempt should be made to twist the spindle out—it is located by two flat surfaces in its housing—but it should be tapped from the outer end, using a rawhide mallet, or a hammer and soft-metal drift.

The final stage in dismantling is to remove the wheel bearings. These are driven out with a soft-metal drift.

Reassembly is fairly straightforward. First, the dust cover is fitted, and then the damper assembly is slipped into its tube—which should be well filled with Jetlube grease—and the valve screwed home. The spring is bolted into place by the top bolt.

For threading the damper rod back into the sliding member a special tool (No. 61–5018) is used. This is screwed to the end of the damper rod, but not locked too tightly. It has the effect of extending the damper rod, and thus making it easier to locate it in its fixing hole.

The damper rod and the spring are guided into the lower member—though before doing this make sure that the shouldered washers have been replaced, or more dismantling will be called for!—the rear domed nut is replaced, and the special tool is removed from the damper rod. That done, the front domed nut is fitted, the damper rod again being held with a screwdriver to prevent rotation.

If the brake cam and the wheel spindle have been removed, these are the next parts to be refitted. Again, the alloy member will need heating to expand the metal sufficiently for the spindle to be replaced. If the fork is off the machine the member can simply be immersed in a bowl of hot water, but if the main fork member is still fitted to the scooter it suffices to

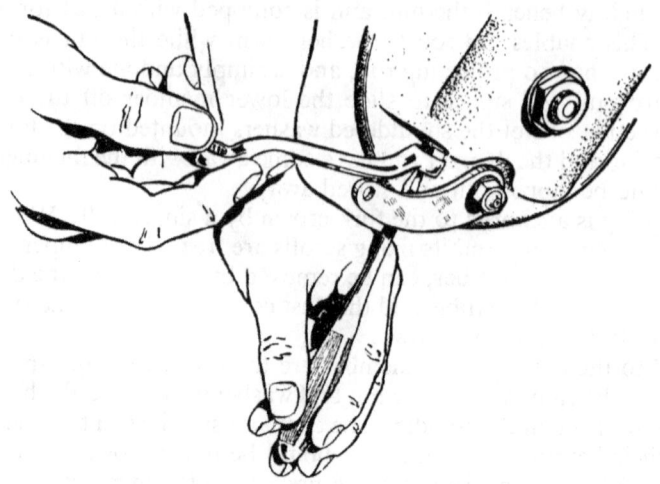

Fig. 20. Removal of the Sliding Member
The damper rod must be held with a screwdriver while the domed nut beneath the fork is undone.

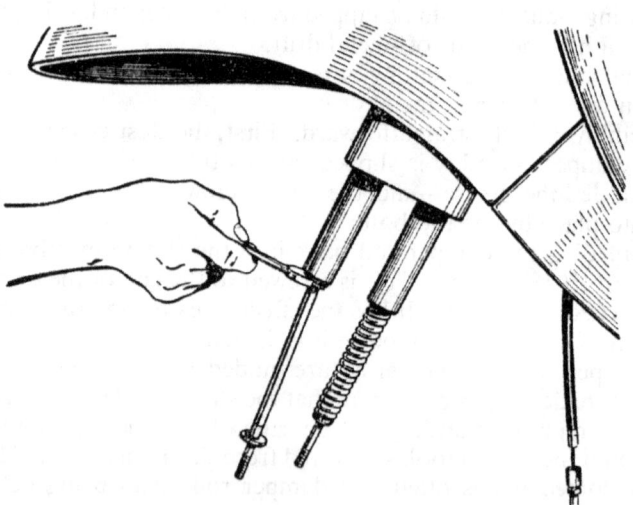

Fig. 21. Removal of the Damper Assembly
It is necessary to unscrew the disc valve from the bottom of the front fork tube.

wring out an old towel in hot water and to wrap it around the sliding member to provide the necessary heat.

Bodywork Removal. If major overhauls are to be carried out, some parts of the bodywork must first be removed. Major engine or transmission work, for example, requires the complete removal of the side valances and the dualseat.

First of all, the two nuts and bolts which hold the C-shaped seat hinges to the seat brackets are removed, and the seat lifted off. The two bolts at the front of the valances are removed, and so is the bolt at the bottom of the rear end. The number plate, on machines not fitted with a carrier, is fastened by two bolts, which must also be taken off the machine. Before the plate itself can be lifted clear, the snap connectors to the rear lamp must be disconnected. On the standard machine, these are usually concealed beneath the rubber tool tray, but where a carrier has been fitted the leads are extended and the connectors may be outside the valances. In this case, the actual lamp lead is concealed by a rubber conduit, and to locate the connectors the conduit is pinched with a finger and thumb along its length until the thicker configuration of the connectors is felt. Then the conduit is pushed forward, along the lamp lead, until the connectors are reached.

There is a further complication when there is also a spare wheel. This is held to the carrier by two nuts, which must be removed. The two bolts, just below the dualseat, which secure the carrier must be loosened and the carrier tilted up to release the spare wheel. Then the two side carrier bolts are completely removed, and the carrier lifted off. The remaining bolts at the rear come off next, leaving only two bolts at each side—a domed and slotted bolt immediately below the seat and a round-headed bolt at the bottom of the valances, just above the pillion passenger's footboard. The dualseat catch knob does not hold the valances, but it has to be unscrewed before the right-hand valance can be removed.

Before removing the bolts holding the left-hand valance on the 175 c.c. model the carburettor choke control has to be freed by removing two nuts. One of these is on the top, and holds the cable to the choke lever; the other secures the cable clip to the rear of the carburettor bell mouth.

It is most unlikely that the front mudguard and front shielding will ever have to be removed, save in the case of severe accidental damage. If it is necessary to replace a dented mudguard, however, removal is a fairly simple job.

It is advisable to have handy a large sack so that the scooter can be laid on its side to give easier access to the securing screws and bolts. First, the Phillips screws—four in number—which are located beneath the mudguard, next to the fork crown, are removed. Next, the nuts securing the mudguard to the small mudguard extensions are released—the bolts have slotted heads—and finally the nuts holding the mudguard to the front shield are removed.

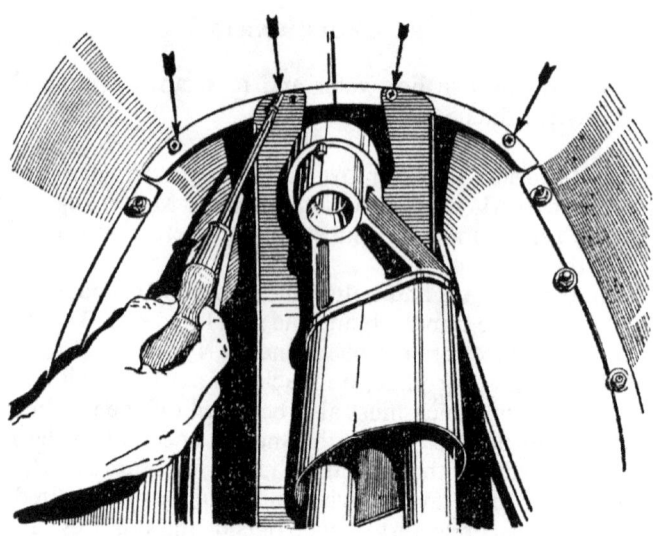

Fig. 22. The Front Panel

This is secured to the mudguard and the mudsplash guard by four screws.

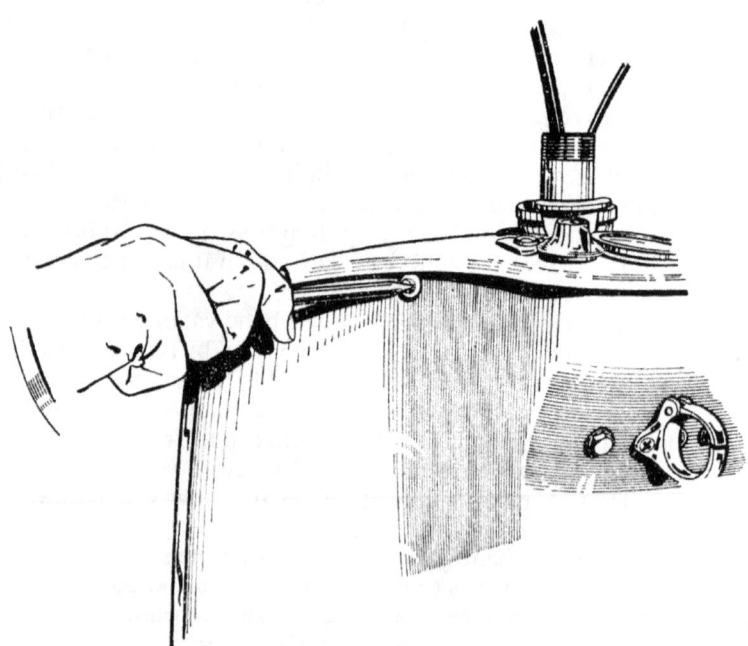

Fig. 23. The Instrument Panel

This is secured by two screws, one on each side of the shielding. These are located in nuts which can only be reached by removing the headlamp.

Alternatively, the mudguard and extension can be removed as one complete unit by undoing the extra bolts which hold the extensions to the underside of the front shield, but leaving the connecting bolts between the mudguard and the extensions secured.

To reach the switchgear and electrical leads in the front shield, the headlamp must be removed. It is held by a single screw, immediately

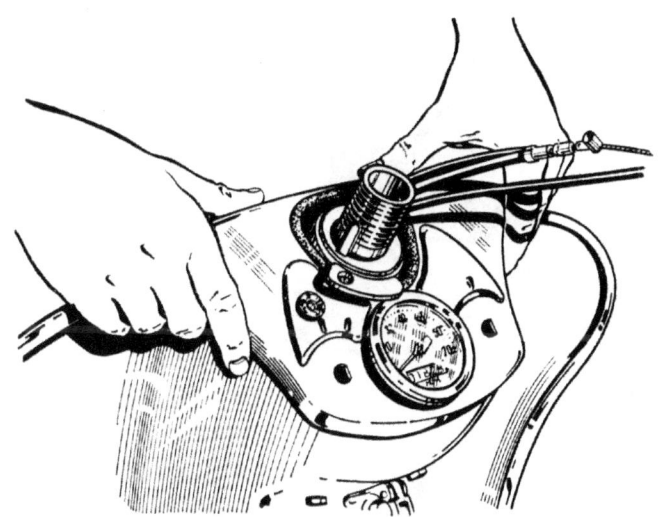

FIG. 24. REMOVAL OF THE INSTRUMENT PANEL
The handlebars must be taken off the machine and the knobs of the switches removed. The speedometer cable is unscrewed from within, access being gained by removing the headlamp.

below the reflector. When the reflector unit has been lifted out, the bulb holder is pressed in and twisted to free the main leads, and the pilot bulb, complete with holder, is pulled from its housing. This enables the reflector to be completely removed from the machine.

Next, the handlebar fairing is detached, and the handlebars removed as described earlier. It is now simply a question of freeing two screws—one on each side of the instrument panel, on the inner face of the front shield. On early models, these screws were fitted into captive nuts, but on most scooters loose nuts and washers are used on the inside of the cowlings, and these are reached through the headlamp nacelle.

Caring for the Bodywork. There is a saying in the motor trade that "polish puts on pounds," and it is certainly true that a scooter, especially, can be badly marred by slapdash cleaning. Conversely, a well cared for machine keeps its value longer than one which has never seen a sponge or a leather.

Cleaning is a simple task, but one with some hidden pitfalls. Of these, the worst is the temptation to "dry clean" the paintwork. In use, the scooter becomes covered with dust, picked up from the air and thrown up from other vehicles. This dust consists of millions of tiny particles, some of which are of very hard substances. If a coating of dust is simply wiped off with a dry rag, the particles are dragged across the paintwork, and the harder ones dig into the paint film, causing scratches. These are minute,

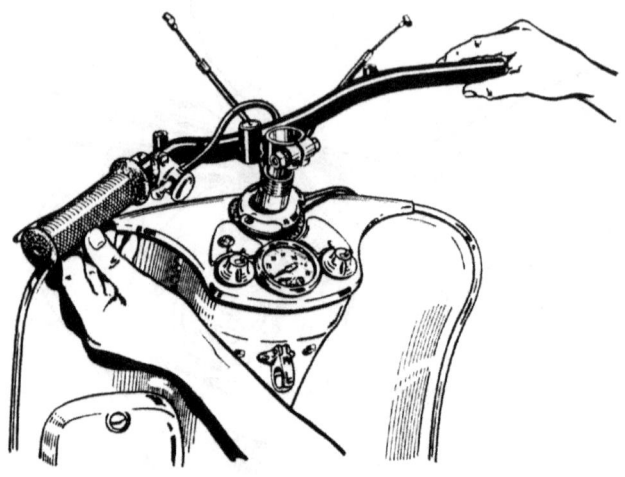

FIG. 25. REPLACING THE HANDLEBAR

The dust cover is fitted over the bearing and followed by the stop plate with the "ears" downwards. When lowering the bar into position it is essential to check that the Woodruff key is a good fit in the fork column.

but also legion, with the result that whole areas of the machine lose their natural shine, and it is only possible to restore it by cutting the paint away to the depth of the scratches—a rather drastic operation.

To clean a scooter, the first essential is plenty of water. This can be applied, gently, with a sponge or soft brush, or by means of a hose. In either case, the operative word is "gently." Furthermore, the water should be generously applied and allowed to soak the dust film.

Once the initial wetting has been done, the dirt is washed away with still more water. This enables it to skid over the surface of the paint without scratching it. Where the machine is really dirty, a certain amount of household detergent can be added to the initial washing water, but plain cold water is almost as good.

When all the dirt has been washed away, the machine should be dried with a chamois leather. This is first of all soaked in water, and then wrung out. It is then placed flat on the bodywork, and drawn along slowly in one straight sweep, absorbing water as it goes. As soon as it is sodden it should be dipped in a bucket of clean water once more, wrung out, and re-applied until the surface water has been completely removed.

Polish nourishes the finish, and after washing and drying a good-quality polish should be applied, using clean mutton cloth. A silicon polish is best, and is also highly economical. Needless to say, only polishes specifically intended for use with synthetic enamels should be used. Metal polish for example, has far too drastic an action to be good for paintwork.

Polish should be applied to small areas at a time, allowed to dry for a few minutes, and then the final shine is given by polishing vigorously with mutton cloth, using quick rotary movements of the hand.

Chromium plating is treated in much the same way. It is often possible to remove incipient rust spots by a vigorous wash with cold water. Here, again, a chamois leather should be employed to dry the parts, and polish applied to finish off. Some of the silicon polishes are suitable for use both on paintwork and on chrome, but it is also possible to obtain special polishes for chromium.

Where the finish has become chipped, and rust has gained a foothold, it is essential that remedial action be taken. Rust has a habit of spreading under the paint film, and this "lifts" the film—in the form of blisters—and so spreads the damage.

First, the affected area is rubbed down with wire wool to remove all rust. In the course of this, adjacent paint areas which have been undermined may also flake off, and these, too, should be well rubbed until only bright clear metal can be seen. Next, a rust-proofing fluid is applied, and then an undercoat of primer must be brushed on. This is important, since coloured synthetic enamels will not adhere to bare metal.

When the primer is dry, it should be rubbed down with wet and dry abrasive paper, and a second undercoat applied if necessary. After the final rubbing down; the synthetic enamel coat can be applied, using the brush in short light strokes to avoid brushmarks.

Although panel beating is an art to which few laymen can aspire, it is possible nowadays to fill bad dents with one of the plastic compounds which are marketed under various trade names.

The paintwork in the dent is sanded down to give a "key," and the filler is made up into a paste of the correct consistency, and applied to the dent rather like putty. It is built up until the dent is filled, and shaped roughly to contour. Then it is allowed to harden—and, believe me, it dries hard and holds tightly! Once hard, it can be sand-papered to give an exact match with the original contours of the panel and smoothed down to give a good surface. It is then primed and painted in exactly the same way as metal.

CHAPTER VII

ROUTINE MAINTENANCE

THERE is, obviously, a difference between routine maintenance—the day to day adjustments and minor repairs which all vehicles need—and major overhauls, but both have their place in keeping a scooter in good working order. Of the two, routine maintenance is actually the more important. A scooter repays constant and sympathetic attention to its everyday condition, but certainly does not appreciate constant stripping of the engine. Many owners, however, fall into the error of neglecting to give their machines minor attention, while ceremoniously pulling them apart two or three times each year.

This is the exact opposite of the correct approach! Well driven and properly maintained, a 250 c.c. B.S.A. "Sunbeam" or Triumph "Tigress" scooter will cover at least 20,000 miles before there is any real need to strip the engine, while the 175 c.c. two-stroke models should call for little more than an occasional "top overhaul" during the same period.

If, however, the routine maintenance is neglected, the time which can elapse between overhauls is drastically shortened, and the amount of work to be done and money to be spent will be greatly increased.

The reason for this is simple enough. Maladjustments have a cumulative effect. Little enough harm is likely to result, for example, if one of the overhead-valve jobs is run with a tight exhaust tappet for a hundred miles before the fault is picked up during a periodic inspection. But if the owner fails to make this routine check, the tight tappet may be left for a thousand, or two thousand miles.

All sorts of troubles can result from this one minor example of neglect. The hot exhaust gases may burn away the seating faces of the valve and the valve insert. The valve stem may be damaged. The engine is unable to develop its full power, since one cylinder never operates at full compression, and this throws a strain on the whole unit. The fuel consumption rises; the performance falls. And, when the fault finally *is* discovered, a complete top overhaul, with a new valve into the bargain, may be necessary. Which is, of course, a pretty stiff price to pay for the minute saved by omitting a weekly tappet check.

An even more glaring example is that of the brakes. The deterioration in braking performance is constant, but very gradual. Consequently, the rider adjusts himself, almost automatically, to the decreasing effectiveness of his brakes, and fails to realize just how much power has been lost until

ROUTINE MAINTENANCE

an emergency stop crops up. This is normally an effective lesson—but it can be a rather dangerous one into the bargain.

TASK SYSTEMS

Constant and methodical inspection is the best way of preventing any such troubles, but the usual recommendations—based on elapsed mileage—are difficult to carry out if a full log of work done is not kept. This was a problem which faced the Armed Forces some years ago, and to combat it the military authorities evolved Task Systems, which called for daily or weekly checks on each aspect of the mechanical side of a vehicle.

In a modified form, such systems are ideally suited for a privately maintained scooter. They can be one of two types—a daily system, or a weekly system. Which is used depends entirely upon the use to which the scooter is put. If it is a "ride-to-work" machine, checks should be made each day. If it is employed solely for weekend excursions, a weekly basis can be substituted.

Taking the daily system first, here is a Task System for the B.S.A. and Triumph machines. It is designed to cover all the major parts which need to be checked, but to carry out these recommendations should never involve the expenditure of more than 10 minutes in a single day, and in most cases only a couple of minutes will be needed.

Daily Task System

Sunday: check adjustment of front and rear brakes; check freedom of action of brake controls; check security of nuts and bolts in braking system; check lubrication of brake cables.
Monday: check oil levels in gearbox, primary gearcase and rear chaincase; on 250 c.c. machines, check oil level in sump; check all controls for free movement and adequate lubrication.
Tuesday: check all exposed electrical wiring for signs of abrasion or fracture; check all electrical terminals for tightness; check operation of lamps and dip switch; check contact-breaker settings.
Wednesday: examine tyre treads and remove any trapped stones; check tyre pressures; check wheels for security; rock wheels and front fork to check play in bearings.
Thursday: check clutch for cable adjustment; check that clutch plates are freeing.
Friday: check all nuts and bolts for security.
Saturday: on 250 c.c. machines, check tappet adjustment; on 175 c.c. and 250 c.c. machines, check sparking plugs for gap and condition; clean and regap if necessary.

Alternative Weekly System

Week 1. Check engine, gearbox, gearcase and chaincase oil levels; check tappet adjustment on 250 c.c. machines; check plugs for gap and condition.

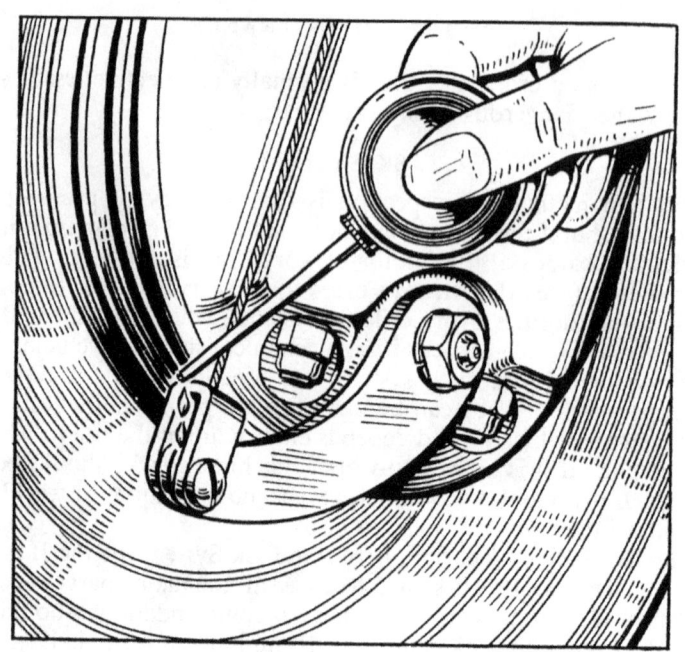

Fig. 26. Oiling the Pivot Pin of the Front Brake Cable
All exposed cables and joints should be oiled weekly using an oil can filled with engine or cycle oil.

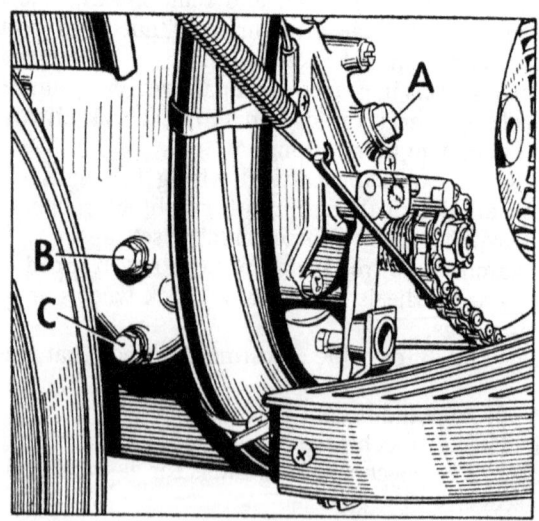

Fig. 27. Three Plugs Used When Lubricating the Gearbox
Plug C is the drain plug through which the used oil is released, and plug A is the filler plug. When the gearbox has been drained and flushed, fresh oil is poured in until it can escape through the hole of plug B which is set at the correct level.

Fig. 28. Checking Tyre Pressures with a Pressure Gauge

Tyre pressures must be kept within the recommended limits, and should be checked with a pressure gauge weekly. The position of the adjuster B and the adjuster lock-nut A for the front brake cable is also shown here.

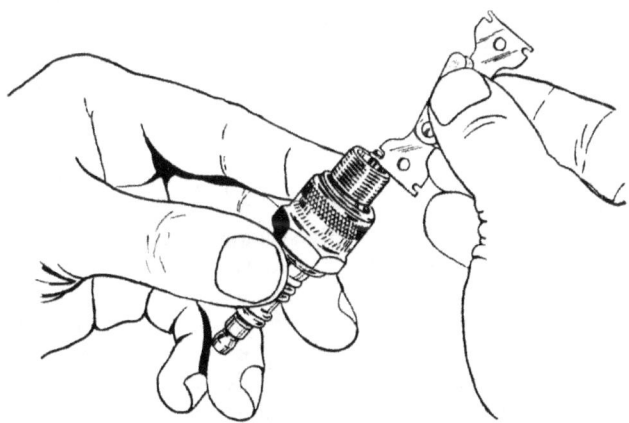

Fig. 29. Regapping a Sparking Plug, using a Sparking Plug Tool which can be bought for a few pence

Week 2. Check brakes for adjustment, freedom of action of controls, and lubrication of cables; check wheels for security; rock wheels and front fork to check play in bearings; examine tyre treads and check tyre pressures.

Week 3. Examine all electrical leads for signs of abrasion or fracture;

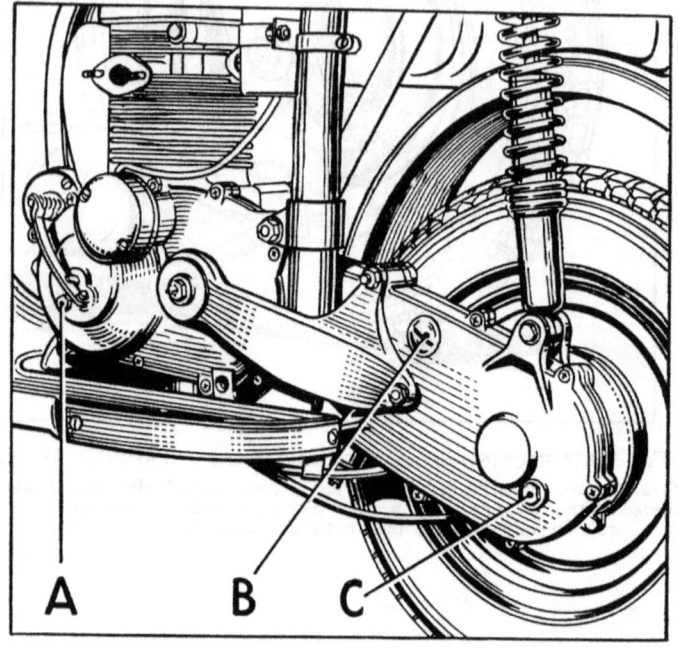

FIG. 30. THE CHAIN CASE PLUGS

The primary chain case has a combined filler and level plug A. On the rear chain case the level plug C is removed, and the oil poured into filler B until it begins to flow from C.

check all terminals for security; check operation of horn, lamps and dip switch; check contact-breaker settings;

Week 4. Check clutch cable for adjustment; check that clutch plates are freeing; check all nuts and bolts for security.

By employing this approach to routine maintenance of the scooter, the rider ensures that most of the major points are checked, by the daily system, at least once each week. Even allowing for a pretty substantial utilization of the machine, this should mean that no fault could go undetected for more than, say, 300 miles, and most defects would be discovered almost before they had had time to develop.

With the weekly system, a month could elapse between the development of a fault and its discovery. Consequently, a weekly inspection system is only really suitable where the distance covered in an average month does not exceed 500 miles.

It is important to note, however, that the idea is to *check* the relevant points, though not necessarily to carry out any actual adjustment. There is no point in adjusting just for the sake of adjusting, and where the

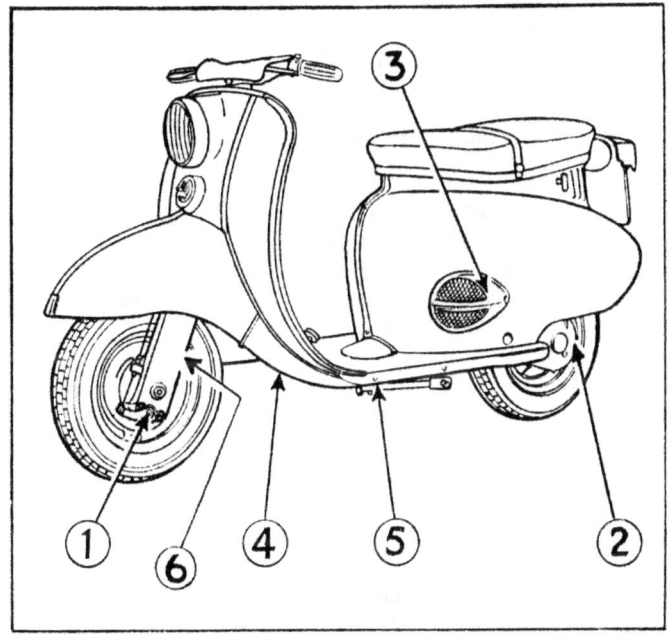

FIG. 31. THE POSITION OF THE SIX GREASE NIPPLES

1. Front brake cam spindle.
2. Rear brake cam spindle.
3. Nearside swinging arm bearing.
4. Foot change pivot pin.
5. Kick-starter pivot spindle.
6. Front fork leg.

routine examination discloses no fault and the adjustment is already correct no actual work should be carried out.

Furthermore, of course, this scheme of daily or weekly spot checks does not take into account such recurrent items as oil changes. These must be done on an elapsed mileage basis, and it is only too easy to forget just when the last change was carried out. Memory—which is notoriously unreliable—can be aided here by sticking to the fuel tank a small strip of self-adhesive coloured tape on which is written the mileage at which the last oil changes were made, or the mileage at which the next *should* be made. Which figures are given is a matter of personal preference.

It is a great mistake to neglect these periodic oil changes, more particularly where the 250 c.c. model is involved. In this unit, the engine oil is contained in a sump and is constantly circulated through the engine. With use, this oil becomes dirty, and also loses some of its power of lubrication. If the oil is not changed at regular intervals, the inside of the engine—including the vital oilways—becomes dirty, and the oil film on the working parts loses its strength and breaks down. Heavy wear then occurs. For this reason, it is vital to change the oil at the stipulated intervals, for these are specified only after exhaustive tests by the manufacturers of the machine.

For much the same reasons, only the recommended grades of oil should be used, and it is inadvisable to mix different brands, even where they are of the correct grade.

MAINTENANCE OF THE 250 c.c. ENGINE

Before checking and adjusting the tappets on the twin-cylinder engine, it is essential to give the unit plenty of time to cool down if it has been run. Ideally, it should be completely cold which, in practice, means that at least five hours must have elapsed since it was last used. Under these conditions, the correct clearance between the rockers and the valve stems is 0·005 in. for both inlet and exhaust valves.

To obtain access to the valves, the sparking plug leads are first detached, and then the two nuts holding the rocker box cover are removed. If the light-alloy cover does not lift off easily and cleanly it should be tapped, very gently, with a block of softwood. This will jar it free without harming the joint washer between the cover and the head which must, of course, be undamaged if it is to form an efficient oil seal. The cowling is fixed separately and need not be taken off.

Next, the sparking plugs should be removed. This enables the engine to be turned over more easily, and it is not at all a bad scheme to examine the plugs at the same time as tappet adjustments are carried out.

Now, the crankshaft is rotated, either by gentle hand pressure on the kick starter, or by engaging gear and turning the rear wheel—until the inclined valve on the left-hand side of the engine is fully depressed by its rocker. At this point, the inclined valve on the right-hand side of the engine is correctly placed for checking.

The actual measurement of the valve clearance is made by sliding the appropriate 0·005 in. feeler horizontally between the valve stem and the tappet. Either it will slide in easily, or it will refuse to enter at all. In the first case, hold the feeler in position and press the end of the rocker with one finger. You should be able to feel no further movement if the setting is correct. As a double check, select the next-highest feeler—probably an 0·008 in. gauge—and try to insert it in place of the 0·005 in. blade. It should not fit. This double check shows that the setting is correct.

If, however, the 0·005 in. feeler when originally tried, refuses to enter the gap, the tappet is too tight and must be loosened. A lock-nut is used to lock the tappet to the rocker in the set position, and the first step in making the adjustment is to loosen this lock-nut slightly. There is no need to undo it completely—in fact, this merely makes the job more difficult. One or two

ROUTINE MAINTENANCE

half-turns with the fingers is enough, once the nut has been unlocked with the tappet spanner supplied in the tool kit.

Now, it is merely a question of unscrewing the adjusting pin until the feeler gauge can just, but only just, slide freely between the end of the pin and the valve stem. Move the feeler backwards and forwards very slightly, and at the same time gently screw down the adjusting pin. The

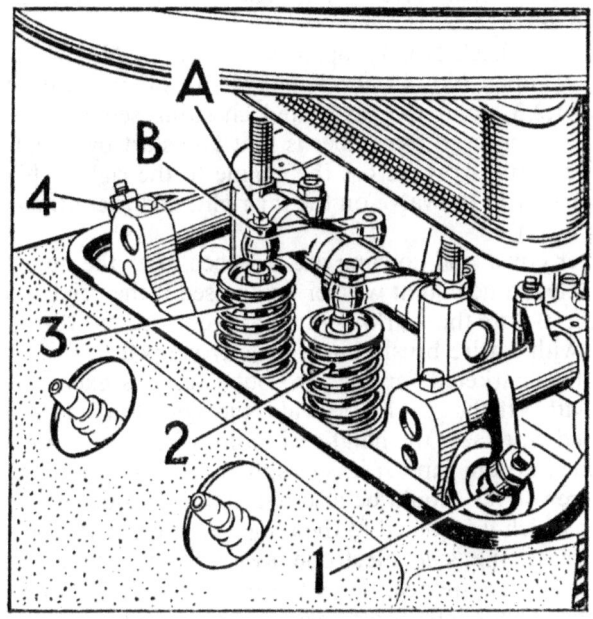

FIG. 32. ADJUSTING THE TAPPETS

The tappets are adjusted by loosening nut B on each rocker in turn and turning the adjusting screw A. The valves are numbered from 1 to 4 reading from the left of the engine to the right.

point at which the feeler blade begins to be trapped by the pin can be distinctly felt. The adjusting pin is then slackened by a fraction of a turn to release the feeler, and this setting is the correct one.

Care must be taken not to "lose" the adjustment as the lock-nut is tightened. The spanners should already be in place on the lock-nut and on the squared end of the adjusting pin. As the lock-nut is tightened, slight opposite pressure should be applied to the spanner holding the adjusting pin, so that the pin cannot be carried round by the lock-nut. As soon as the lock-nut has been tightened, the tappet setting must be re-checked to make certain that it has not been altered.

The same procedure is employed for all the remaining tappets. Once again, the engine is rotated until the left-hand valve of the vertical pair of valves is fully open, when the other vertical valve can be checked. This valve, in turn, is then brought to the fully open position, and the left-hand vertical valve checked. Finally, the inclined valve on the right-hand side is opened, and the setting of the inclined valve on the left-hand side ascertained.

If the valves are regarded as being numbered from left to right, the inclined valve on the left will be No. 1, the vertical valves Nos. 2 and 3, and the right-hand inclined valve No. 4. The checking sequence can then be remembered as—

Open No. 1—check No. 4; open No. 2—check No. 3; open No. 3—check No. 2; open No. 4—check No. 1. In other words, the opening sequence is 1,2,3,4 and the associated checking sequence 4,3,2,1. This means that all you need remember is that you start by opening the valve on the far left, and work across the engine to the right, while the actual checking starts with the valve on the far right, and is continued across the engine to the left.

The rocker cover and cowling are replaced after the adjustments have been completed, a new joint washer being used if the original has suffered any damage. Before the sparking plugs are replaced, however, they should be cleaned with a wire brush, and correctly gapped to 0·020/0·025 in. A special tool is marketed for the job, but if care is exercised it is easily dispensed with. If the gap is too wide, the side electrode should be very gently tapped with, say, the handle of a screwdriver until the feeler gauge will just slide into the gap. If it is less than the minimum, the blade of an electrical screwdriver should be inserted under the side electrode, close to the point at which it is joined to the plug body, and a very gentle pressure exerted to ease the side electrode away from the central electrode. Remember that you are dealing with a matter of a few thousandths of an inch, and that only gentle force needs to be applied.

When replacing the sparking plugs, beware of over-tightening. Each plug has a copper/asbestos sealing washer, which *must* be replaced. This not only forms the joint between the plug and the head, but also controls to some extent the "reach" of the plug in the combustion chamber. The plug must be tightened just sufficiently to crush this washer between its own body and the head, but not so tightly that the washer is completely flattened. Excessive force used in replacing a sparking plug can damage the threads in the head, and can also distort the body of the plug, thus causing air leaks. The best method is to tighten the plug by hand, as far as possible, before slipping a box spanner over it to give the final few turns. As the plug is tightened, the point at which the washer is trapped can be felt, and it is then sufficient to give an extra half-turn with the spanner to form a perfect seal. This, incidentally, should be a smooth hand movement—not a sudden jerk of the whole arm. Where the washers are badly crushed, it is best to replace them with new ones, since with flattened washers not only is this correct tightening procedure impossible, but it is also very difficult indeed to obtain an efficient seal.

ROUTINE MAINTENANCE 69

Just as the sparking plugs must be correctly gapped if the full efficiency of the electrical system is to be brought to bear, so too must the contact-breaker points be properly set. There is one set of points for each cylinder on the "250," and in both cases the correct gap between the points, when fully open, is 0·015 in.

To reach the contact-breaker, the inspection cover on the left-hand side of the bodywork must be removed. This is held by a single screw at the

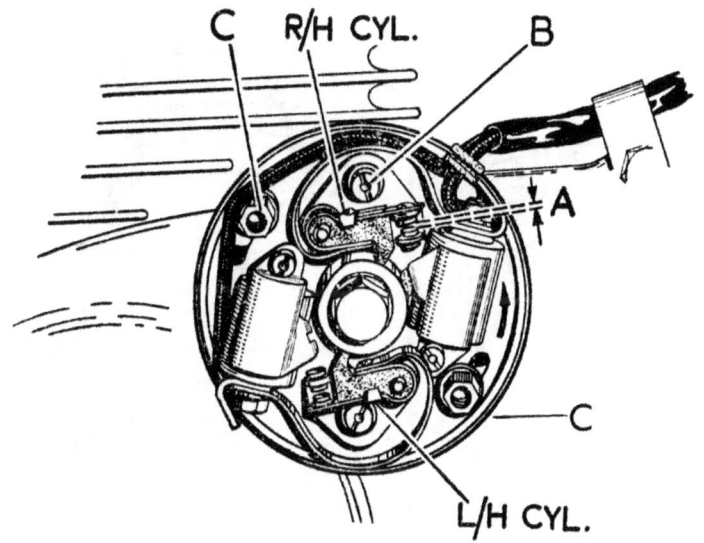

FIG. 33. THE DISTRIBUTOR OF THE 250 C.C. MODEL WITH THE CAP REMOVED SHOWING THE TWIN CONTACT-BREAKERS

The gap A must be maintained accurately at 0·015 in. It is adjusted by loosening the nut B of each breaker in turn, and moving the contact-breaker plate until the gap is correct. The two nuts C hold the entire stator plate, and should not be touched unless the timing itself is to be altered.

rear, and by a tongue at the front. Inside, the contact-breaker is mounted behind a cover, just above the clutch operating arm. Two screws secure this cover, and inside are the two contact-breaker assemblies with their two condensers. The contact-breakers are operated by a cam in the centre, and this is fitted with a wick-type lubricator which keeps the surface of the cam lightly smeared with grease.

Whenever the points are checked, first ensure that this wick is not dry. It should have the slightly greyish and damp appearance which is characteristic of moistened felt, but it should not be over-soaked with grease or the surplus may reach the points and cause burning.

To check the points gap, rotate the engine slowly and watch the upper contact-breaker. The point of maximum opening comes when its fibre arm is seated on the peak of the revolving cam. The points gap is then measured, and the points themselves inspected. They should be clean; set squarely to each other; and show no signs of pitting or burning on their mating faces.

Dirty points should be cleaned before being set. A piece of non-fluffy cloth soaked in petrol, and inserted between the points with a knife blade, will soon get rid of excess dirt. To dry the points afterwards, the cam is moved on until the points just close. The arm is then lifted sufficiently for

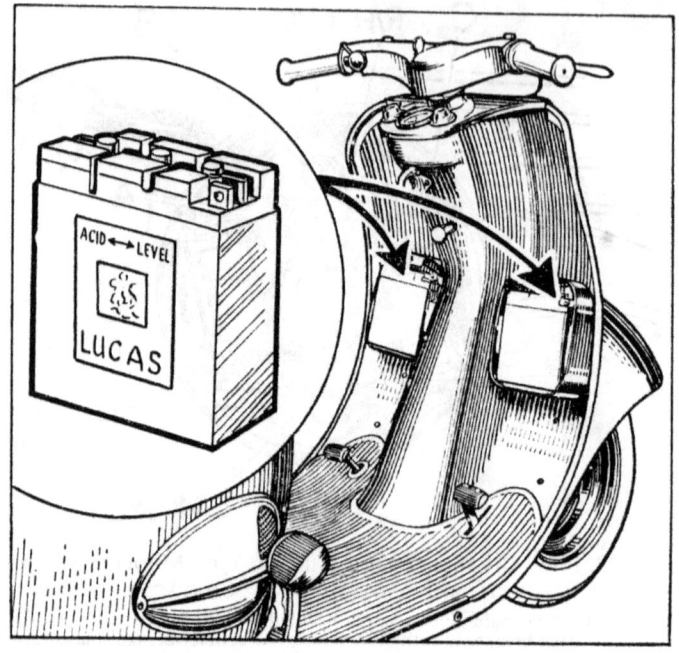

FIG. 34. THE BATTERIES
Each battery has an acid level mark and at least once every fortnight the battery should be inspected to ensure that the level is maintained. Distilled water is needed for topping-up.

a clean piece of paper to be slipped between the points, and they are allowed to snap shut upon it. It is then slowly and carefully withdrawn against the pressure of the points. Repeated once or twice, this completes the cleaning process. Points which are pitted, or worn at an angle, should either be filed flat and square with a special points file, or else replaced completely.

If, however, the points pass muster when inspected at the fully open position the only work to be done is to measure the gap, and reset it if necessary. The fixed point is carried on a plate, which is locked by a single screw. This screw is loosened—not very much; just enough to

ROUTINE MAINTENANCE

allow the plate to be moved—and the plate repositioned to give the correct gap. It is then held securely while the screw is retightened, and as soon as this has been done the gap is re-checked. Exactly the same procedure is employed for the remaining set of points.

On the other side of the electrical system—the lighting circuit—an eye should be kept on the condition of the battery or batteries, depending upon the model. Transparent cases are employed on these batteries, and since the only job to be done is to keep an eye on the level of the electrolyte this is almost literally a check which can be made "at a glance."

On each case is a blue line, and this marks the level at which the acid should be maintained to fill and soak the M.L.Z. 9E battery. Each cell is filled to the line with dilute sulphuric acid of the appropriate specific gravity, and the battery allowed to stand for one hour.

For filling both uncharged and dry charged batteries the specific gravity of the electrolyte (corrected to 60°F or 15·5°C) is 1·270 s.g. in climates with a temperature normally below 90°F, or 1·210 s.g. in climates above 90°F.

To maintain the level thereafter, top up to the line with distilled water. Tap water should never be used for battery-topping, since it contains impurities which may cause damage to the battery. In an emergency, however, it is permissible to use water obtained by defrosting a domestic refrigerator.

MAINTENANCE OF THE 175 c.c. ENGINE

Since a two-stroke engine has no valves to check, the routine maintenance of the 175 c.c. model is even simpler than the none-too-exacting work necessary to maintain the 250 c.c. job in good order. In fact, it boils down to keeping the sparking plug clean and correctly gapped, and to keeping the contact-breaker points in good condition.

So far as the sparking plug is concerned, its maintenance is similar in every detail to that of the "250," described on page 68, with the rider that the two-stroke plug is more likely to be fouled, owing to the greater quantity of oil present in the combustion chamber. For this reason, it is best to have the plug sand-blasted at a garage at regular intervals, since this is the only sure method of cleaning oily deposits out of the body of the plug. Whenever this is done, however, it is essential that the plug should be thoroughly air-blasted afterwards, before it is refitted. This is to ensure that no sand remains trapped in the plug, for if such grains found their way into the engine the cylinder bore could be badly scratched.

To reach the contact-breaker points, the grilled inspection cover on the right-hand valance is removed by undoing its single fixing screw. In the face of the flywheel several slots are cut. These are concealed by a cover plate, held by four screws. This plate is removed and the wheel revolved until the contact-breaker mechanism can easily be seen. Slight movements of the flywheel, backwards and forwards, will enable you to gauge when the

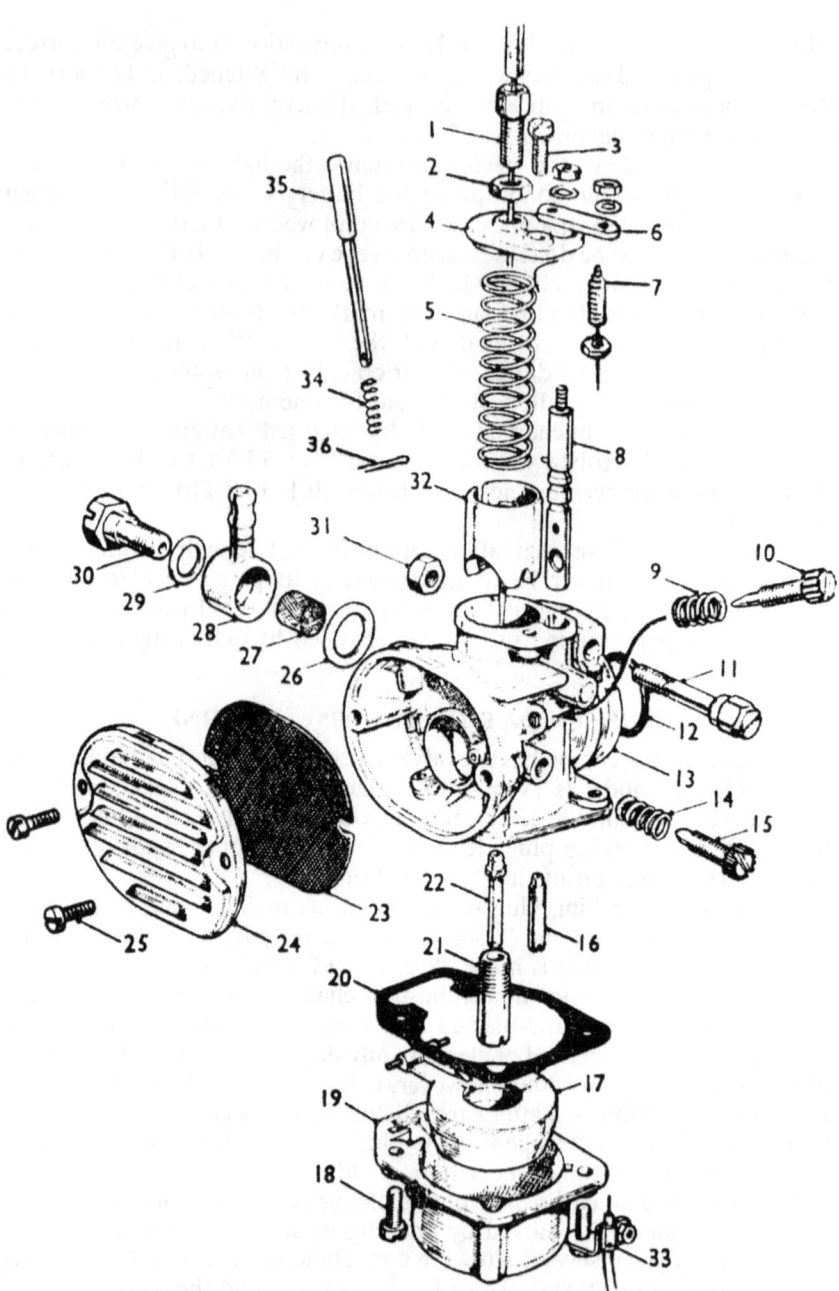

Fig. 35. The Zenith Carburettor as Used on the 250 c.c. Machine

ROUTINE MAINTENANCE

points are fully open, and the gap between them should be measured in the normal way. Cleaning, if necessary, should be carried out as described on page 70, and regapping then follows.

The fixed point is carried on a plate which is locked by a cheese-head screw. A smaller screw, operating in a slot, gives the necessary means of

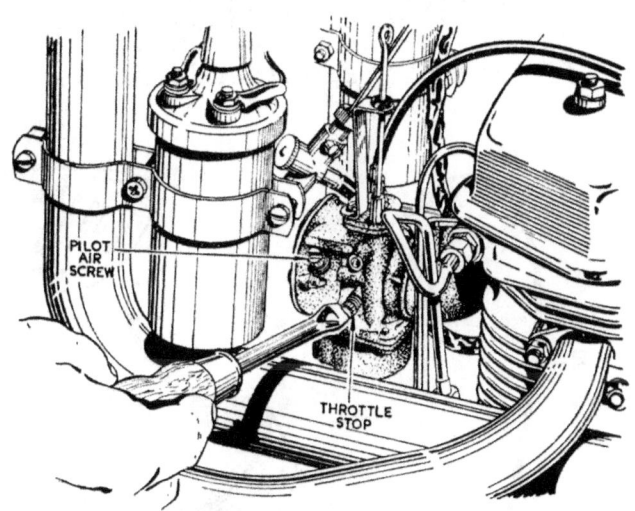

FIG. 36. TICK-OVER REGULATING SCREWS

Except for the earliest models, all the 250 c.c. machines have two screws on the carburettor for regulating the tick-over. The throttle stop and the pilot air screw must be balanced, as described in the text.

adjustment. When the locking screw has been slackened, the adjuster screw is turned with a screwdriver until the gap between the points is 0·020 in. While the adjusting screw is still held, the large, round-headed

---

KEY TO FIG. 35

1. Cable adjuster.
2. Lock-nut for cable adjuster.
3. Cover plate screw.
4. Cover plate.
5. Spring, main slide.
6. Choke operating arm.
7. Choke cable anchor.
8. Starter slide.
9. Spring, pilot air screw.
10. Pilot air screw.
11. Clamping screw.
12. "O" ring.
13. Carburettor body.
14. Spring, throttle adjustment screw.
15. Throttle adjustment screw.
16. Slow running jet.
17. Float.
18. Carburettor bowl screw (2).
19. Carburettor bowl.
20. Gasket.
21. Main jet.
22. Emulsion tube.
23. Air-intake gauze.
24. Cover for air-intake gauze.
25. Cover screw (2).
26. Filter elbow washer.
27. Filter gauze.
28. Filter banjo.
29. Filter plug washer.
30. Filter plug.
31. Clamping screw nut.
32. Main slide and needle.
33. Choke outer cable securing clip.
34, 35, 36. Tickler assembly.

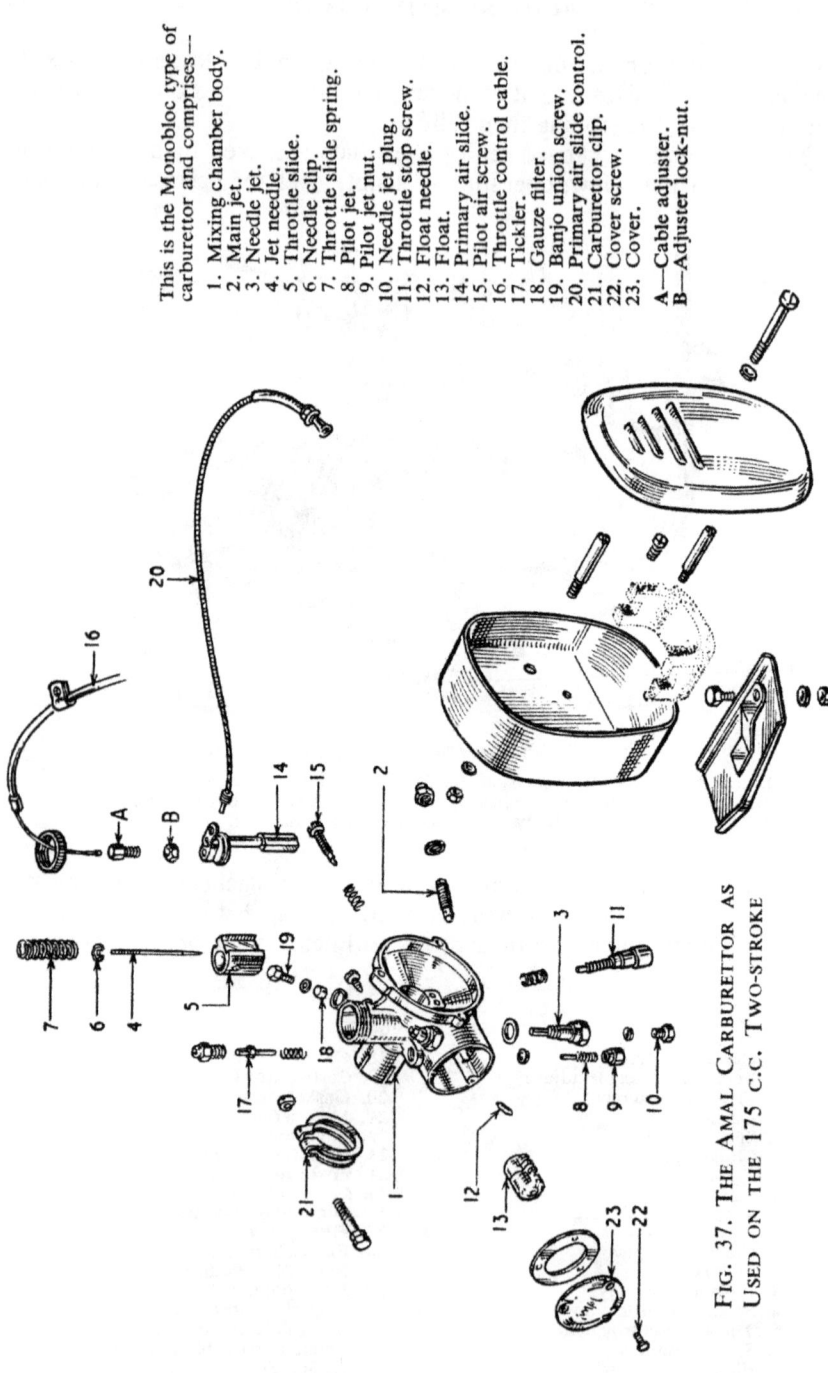

This is the Monobloc type of carburettor and comprises—

1. Mixing chamber body.
2. Main jet.
3. Needle jet.
4. Jet needle.
5. Throttle slide.
6. Needle clip.
7. Throttle slide spring.
8. Pilot jet.
9. Pilot jet nut.
10. Needle jet plug.
11. Throttle stop screw.
12. Float needle.
13. Float.
14. Primary air slide.
15. Pilot air screw.
16. Throttle control cable.
17. Tickler.
18. Gauze filter.
19. Banjo union screw.
20. Primary air slide control.
21. Carburettor clip.
22. Cover screw.
23. Cover.
A—Cable adjuster.
B—Adjuster lock-nut.

Fig. 37. The Amal Carburettor as Used on the 175 c.c. Two-stroke

screw is tightened to lock the points at the correct setting, which is subsequently re-checked.

Carburettor Adjustments, 175 c.c. and 250 c.c. Models.

Although the correct settings are more or less "built in" to the carburettors when the machines leave the factory, as the mileage mounts it is possible that the pilot air bleed screws and the throttle stop may need adjustment to give a faster or slower tick-over.

On the Zenith carburettor fitted to the 250 c.c. model, the pilot air screw is mounted, in an inclined position, high up on the carburettor bell mouth, and the throttle stop screw is fitted horizontally on the side of the mixing chamber. Both are on the right-hand side of the engine. Some early models had only a throttle stop.

The 175 c.c. model has an Amal Monobloc carburettor, and here the throttle stop is mounted in an inclined position low down on the mixing chamber, and the pilot air bleed screw horizontally, just behind the mixing chamber. Again, both are on the right-hand side of the engine.

Finding the combination of settings which will give a reasonably slow and reliable tick-over calls for patience, and a good "ear." The machine is placed on the stand and the engine allowed to run until it is warmed up.

With the Zenith carburettor, the pilot control should be slowly screwed in—about one eighth of a turn at a time—and a few seconds allowed to elapse while the effect of the adjustment on the engine speed is noted. Screwing-in the control richens the mixture, and slows down the engine. Screwing the throttle stop screw outwards lowers the throttle slide, and also slows the engine. When further turning of the pilot control causes the engine to run with a "lumpy" sound, the screw should be slackened by about a quarter of a turn, and the throttle stop adjusted to give the required rate of tick-over. The throttle should then be opened sharply. If the engine picks up without hesitation, and with no tendency to gulp and cut out on any part of the throttle range, the settings are correct. If cutting out occurs, the pilot control must be readjusted slightly until the pick-up is clean, and the throttle stop then reset to give the slowest reliable tick-over. This is somewhat difficult to achieve, as the Zenith controls are rather coarse, and a delicate touch is necessary.

With the Amal carburettor, the engine is run until it is warm, and then stopped. The pilot screw is turned until it is fully home, and is then released by one-and-a-half turns. The throttle stop screw is loosened until the throttle valve is fully closed.

The engine is now restarted, and the throttle opened to give a fast idling speed. This is held while the throttle stop screw is tightened sufficiently to hold this fast tick-over.

Next, the throttle stop screw is racked out, slowing the tick-over until the engine begins to falter. Now screw the pilot screw in or out until the engine runs without faltering, then blip the throttle to check the pick-up.

Unscrew the throttle stop again until the engine falters once more; then repeat the pilot screw adjustment and the test of opening up. The desired slow running should have been attained by now, but if not the procedure can be carried out once more.

As a refinement of this procedure, the throttle slide can be pulled out of the body, and the throttle needle placed in its lowest groove. If, under

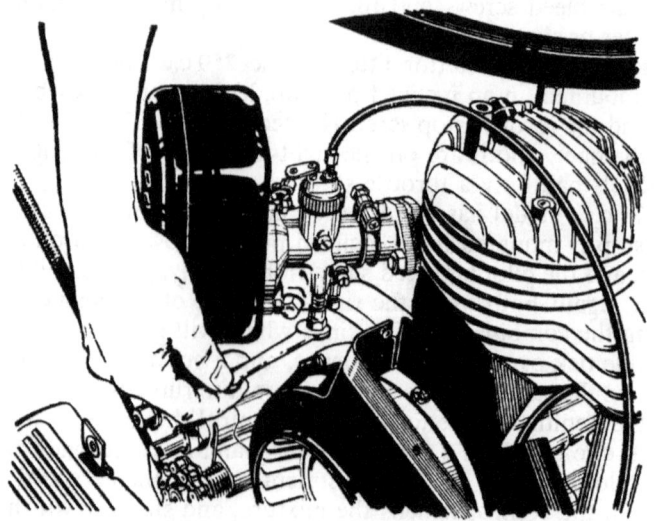

FIG. 38. THE THROTTLE STOP ON THE 175 C.C. MODEL
This should be adjusted with a spanner.

load, the engine subsequently spits back through the carburettor, or the acceleration is poor, the needle should be raised two notches, and the scooter again tested. If a considerable improvement is noted, the needle can again be lowered by a single notch. After these tests, the final position of the needle can be decided. It should be placed in whichever notch gave the best results. Afterwards, if this is different from its original position, the slow running should again be re-adjusted.

Clutch and Gear Adjustment. The clutch has two enemies—slip and drag. When the clutch slips, the friction plates continually rub against each other, and the heat so generated may be sufficient to burn away the linings, and render the clutch wholly inoperative. When the clutch drags, the plates never free fully, and gearchanging becomes extremely difficult.

On both 175 c.c. and 250 c.c. models, two sets of clutch adjustment are provided. One is a cable adjustment, which is used to regulate the amount of play in the control mechanism, and the other is spring adjustment, which regulates the force exerted by the clutch springs on the plates.

On a correctly-adjusted clutch, the first $\frac{1}{8}$ in. of movement when the

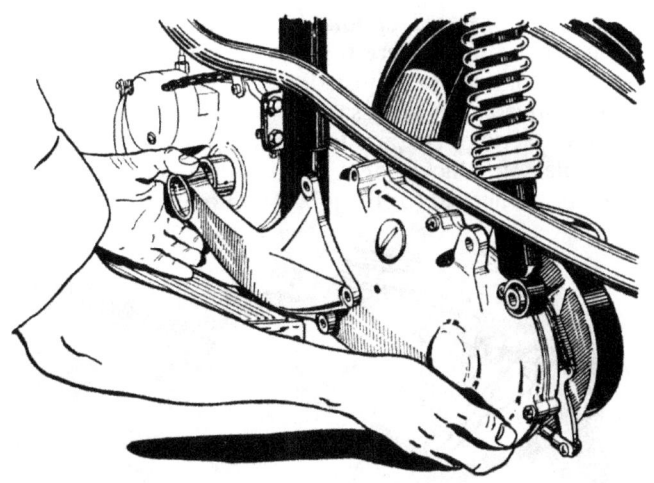

Fig. 39. Renewal of the Clutch Plates

The side valances must first be removed, then take off the curved support arm on the rear chain case.

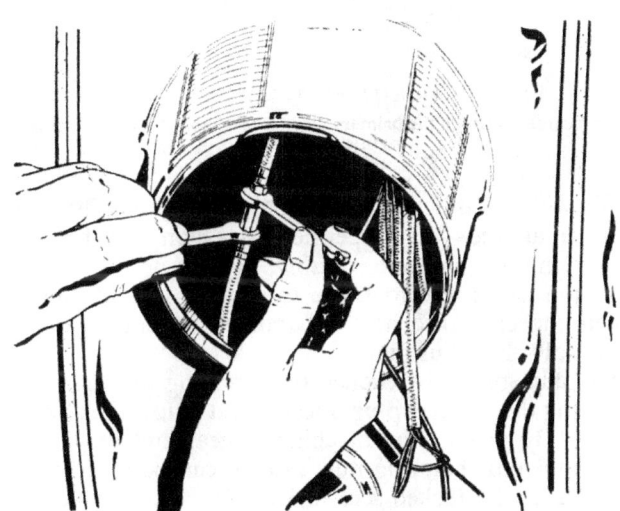

Fig. 40. The Clutch Cable Adjuster

This is located just behind the headlamp which must be removed to allow the adjuster to be used. The throttle cable adjuster is also reached in this way.

handlebar lever is operated should be free. This is a built-in safety measure to prevent slip. Where this play is not present—or where it is exceeded—the cable must be adjusted.

To reach the adjuster it is necessary to remove the headlamp. Inside the shell, beside the steering head, are two cables, both with adjusters. One is the throttle cable; the thicker of the two is the clutch cable.

Two spanners are needed for the job. With one, the base of the adjuster

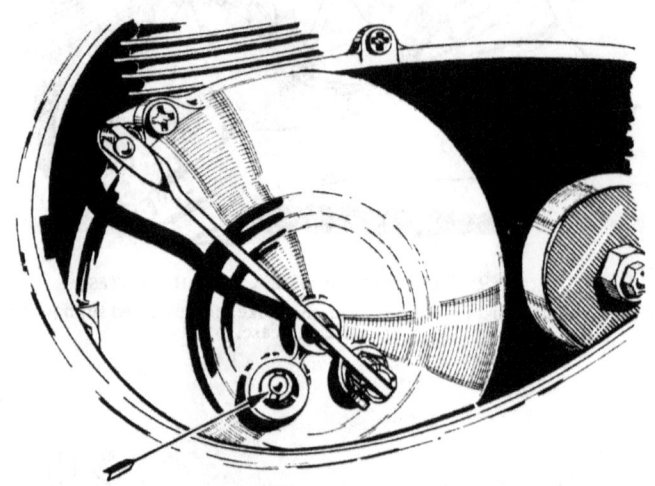

FIG. 41. TIGHTENING THE CLUTCH SPRINGS
This can be done through the primary case oil level hole. A forked screwdriver is required for the job.

is held while with the other the lock-nut is loosened. Then the adjuster's length can be altered—the uppermost hexagon can be screwed anti-clockwise to lengthen the outer casing, and so decrease the amount of free play at the lever; or clockwise to shorten it, and thus increase the play. When the clearance at the handlebar is correct the lock-nut is tightened to hold the adjustment.

The spring adjustment is reached by removing the nearside grille, and then unscrewing the oil level plug, located just below the clutch rod on the primary case. By placing the machine in gear and moving it forwards, each of the three clutch spring nuts in turn can be brought opposite the inspection hole, and a forked screwdriver placed in the slots can be used to tighten each one. Count the number of turns given, and adjust each nut equally. Uneven adjustment means uneven withdrawal, and the plates will rub at one point unless the withdrawal is absolutely even.

Another method of locating the nuts is to insert a screwdriver, which is pressed lightly against the clutch. The kick starter is then gently operated by hand, until you feel a nut come into contact with the screwdriver.

Very occasionally, it may be necessary to reset the length of the rod linking the footboard gear control with the gearbox. This should be done if the gears fail to engage properly when the control is operated.

The first step is to disconnect the rod from the control pedal by taking out the fulcrum pin. Then engage first gear by pressing the gear lever on the gearbox in the direction of the rear wheel, rocking the scooter to and fro slightly to ease the engagement as you do so. This lever must be held

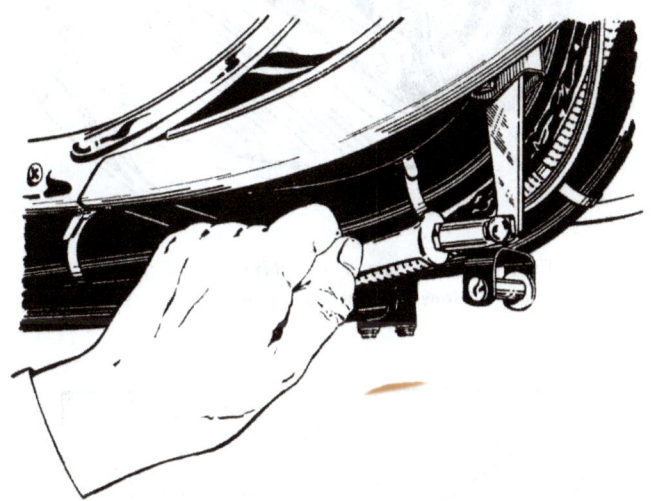

FIG. 42. THE POSITION OF THE GEAR CONTROL ROD
This must have its length adjusted if the gearchange becomes difficult.

back in the engagement position—an aero-elastic strap forms a useful "third hand" here—and the control pedal is moved to the first-gear position and held fully forward. The lock-nut on the gear control rod is slackened, and the coupling screwed out until the coupling holes just coincide with the hole in the pedal. The fulcrum pin is then refitted, and the lock-nut retightened.

The neutral finder, too, may require to be adjusted, and this is a job which should be done when the side valances have been removed, since it requires access to the gearbox. First, slacken the pinch bolt which is located on the reverse side of the gear operating lever, trapping the end of the neutral finder control wire. The gear pedal is now operated to select true neutral—i.e., the neutral position between first and second gears. The gear lever on the gearbox must then be pressed forward towards the second gear position as far as possible, but without actually engaging second gear, and it is held in this position while the pinch bolt is retightened. This should leave approximately a quarter of an inch of wire showing past the swivel on the gear lever.

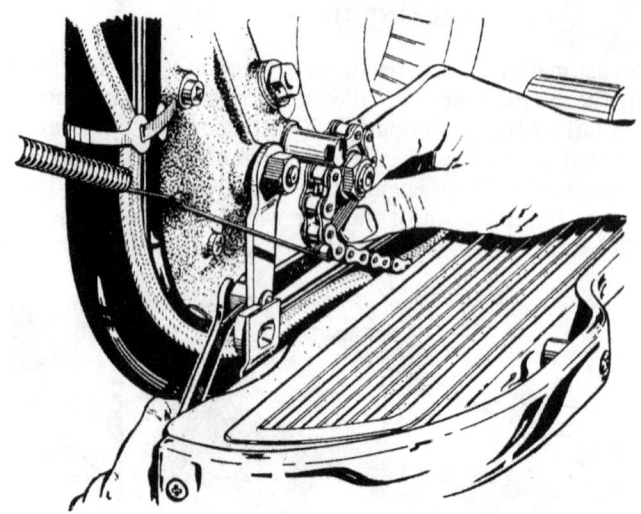

Fig. 43. Resetting the Neutral Finder
This can only be done after the side valances have been removed.

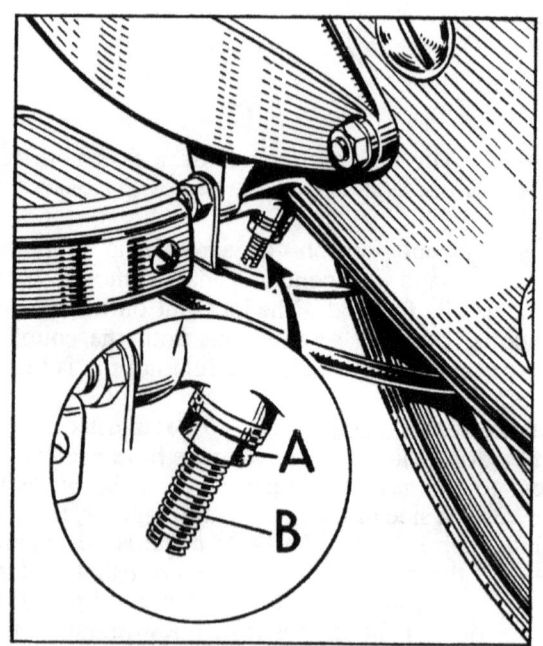

Fig. 44. The Chain Adjustment Screw
The chain is adjusted by means of the screw B located beneath the chain case. It is locked by a lock nut A.

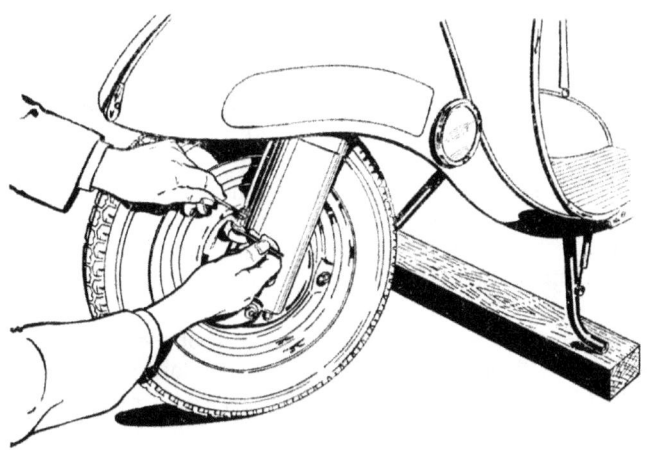

FIG. 45. THE FRONT BRAKE

This is the more effective of the two, and must be kept in adjustment. The scooter wheel should be raised off the ground to facilitate checking and wear taken up on the cable adjuster.

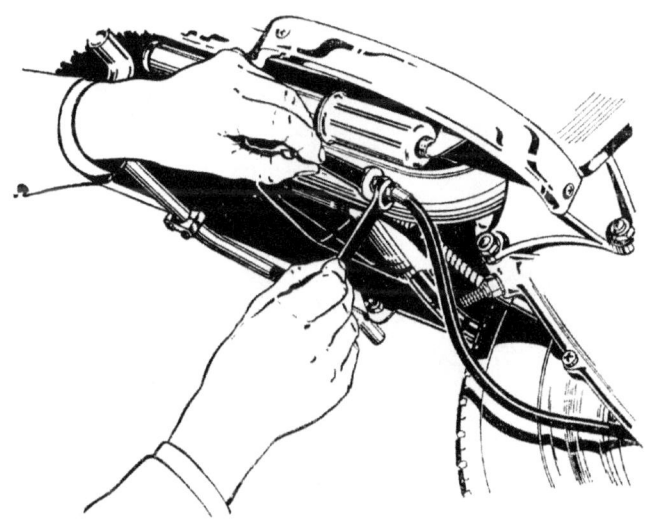

FIG. 46. THE REAR BRAKE CABLE ADJUSTER

This is located under the left footboard. The tyre pump is also mounted here.

Rear Chain Adjustment. An unpleasantly harsh feeling in the transmission is a pretty sure sign that the adjustment of the rear chain has been neglected. Besides being bad for the transmission, incorrect adjustment at this point may lead to bad gearchanging.

The chain tension can be checked through the inspection cap in the rear chain case, merely by inserting a finger under the top run of the chain and feeling how much up and down "play" exists. It should be no more than a quarter of an inch but, at the same time, the chain should not be absolutely tight.

The adjustment is made by means of a slipper-type tensioner at the bottom of the chain case. The lock-nut must be slackened, and the adjuster screw is then screwed inwards to tighten the chain, or outwards to slacken it. Once the correct amount of play has been obtained, the adjuster is held securely while the lock-nut is retightened.

Brake Adjustment. Both front and rear brakes are cable-operated, and adjustment is by means of cable adjusters.

At the front, the adjuster is mounted on the light-alloy sliding fork member. To take up play, this adjuster is racked out, the exact amount being determined by frequent dabs on the front brake lever. The brake should be fully on when the lever is approximately half way back to the bar.

The rear brake adjuster is located on the left-hand side of the machine, immediately below the passenger's footboard. This adjuster should be racked out until the brake pedal stops $1\frac{1}{2}$ in. from the footboard when the brake is fully applied.

CHAPTER VIII

MAJOR OVERHAULS

GIVEN the tools, the necessary mechanical knowledge, and a reasonable workshop in which to carry out the work, there is no reason why the private owner should not do almost any job on his scooter himself. However, scooters are more akin to modern cars than to motor-cycles, in that they are designed and constructed more as a complete mechanical unit. This, in turn, means that although ample facilities have been provided for all necessary routine adjustments, major work often entails the complete removal of the engine/transmission unit from the machine, and subsequent stripping may involve several components and will almost certainly call for the use of special tools.

From the private owner's point of view, the governing factor must be whether or not it is worthwhile tackling any given job himself. Since some of the operations are quite complicated and may take up a considerable amount of time if the man doing the job is not a trained mechanic, the answer should generally be "No!" The main object behind doing one's own maintenance is to save time and money. Where there is no appreciable saving in either, and there is in addition the risk of getting completely out of one's depth and possibly ruining a few components for good measure, then "doing it yourself" is simply defeating its own object. It is, in fact, just as important to know what *not* to do as it is to know how to carry out the jobs that *are* within the average rider's compass.

For this reason, the scope of this chapter has been deliberately restricted to include only those jobs which can be done at home by anybody with average mechanical ability. The minority of enthusiasts who wish to delve deeper into the subject can, however, obtain from the manufacturers an excellent range of Service Sheets and Service Charts which deal exhaustively and clearly with more advanced work on the 175 and 250 c.c. scooters, and which detail the various special tools and techniques required for a complete strip-down.

Of the major jobs, perhaps the one which most owners place highest on the list is decarbonizing—or, at least, top overhauls. There is a considerable danger, however, that this job can be done much too frequently—a hang-over, perhaps, from days—now long past—when engines needed this attention every couple of thousand miles.

This is by no means the case to-day. Advances in metallurgy, in the design and engineering of power units, and in the blending and refining of oils and fuels have altered the picture completely. Engines can now run for many thousands of miles without being decarbonized—or could do, if only their owners would allow it!

Decarbonizing is *not* a magic cure-all which has to be applied to an engine at rigid mileage intervals. Where an engine is running properly, it should be left alone. Every time it is stripped, and subsequently re-assembled, fresh stresses are set up; well-made joints are broken; and the general running of the unit is affected. It may take anything up to a further thousand miles for the engine to settle down—at which point, of course, our amateur mechanic is just on the point of stripping it again!

An engine is, in fact, rather like your own body. It needs periodic minor attention, but it does not appreciate frequent major surgery. If your doctor specified an operation every time you caught a cold in the head it is doubtful if you would survive very long—and the same applies to the scooter engine. So long as it is running smoothly, developing its proper power and not using an excessive amount of either fuel or oil, then all the work which is either desirable or necessary is the simple routine set out in the previous chapter, plus the usual oil changes. When the fuel consumption or oil consumption rises; when the power falls; or the engine begins to feel rough; then there is justification for opening it up to see what the trouble is.

DECARBONIZING THE 175 c.c ENGINE

Before decarbonizing, it is advisable to obtain a top overhaul gasket set (No. 00-3124) and a supply of clean engine oil. In addition to the normal tool kit, it will also be necessary to have scrapers for removing carbon. These can either be professional scrapers, obtainable from tool shops, or a home-made substitute, such as a stick of solder filed into a wedge shape at one end, or a similarly-shaped piece of soft-wood. A couple of boxes lined with clean newspaper will be needed to receive parts removed from the machine, and some clean, non-fluffy rag should also be handy.

First, the side valances are removed. Then the fuel pipe should be disconnected from the carburettor by removing the single bolt in the banjo union. After slackening the pinch bolt on the carburettor clip the carburettor, complete with its air filter, can be eased off the inlet stub, and placed out of the way of the cylinder.

Next, detach the high-tension lead, and take out the two quarter-inch bolts which hold the air trunking to the cylinder head. The left-hand bolt also serves to secure the support bracket of the petrol tap, and this can be swung to one side. On the right of the engine, three $\frac{3}{16}$ in. screws hold the ducting to the fan casing.

Once dismantling has reached this stage, it is as well to clean the outside of the engine before going further. Use a paint brush to spread degreasing fluid over the head, barrel and crankcase, and then hose off the dirt, using only a gentle flow of water. Dry the unit with rag before carrying on.

Remove the four nuts which hold the cylinder head, and place them—

FIG. 47. DECARBONIZING THE 175 C.C. MACHINE
After removing the side valances remove the carburettor and air filter.

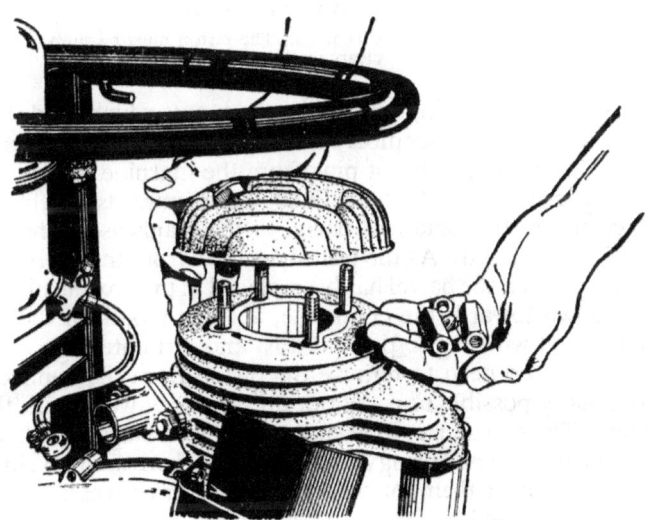

FIG. 48. THE FOUR NUTS WHICH SECURE THE HEAD
The rear nuts are longer than the front ones.

together with their washers—in one of the boxes. Try to place them in order, so that when reassembling commences they can be refitted in their original place. A mark with a soft lead pencil, or with chalk, can be made on each one to show which is which.

At the base of the cylinder, passing through the crankcase, are two screws with slotted Phillips heads. These must be slackened. Next,

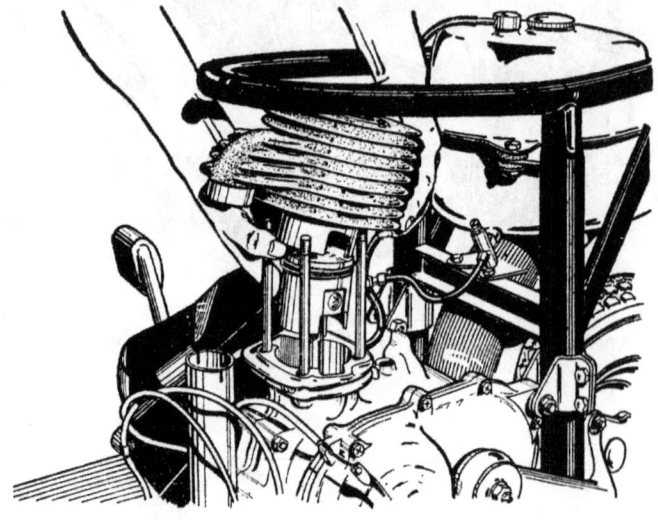

FIG. 49. REMOVAL OF THE BARREL
The barrel is pulled upwards off its studs. The piston must be supported as it clears the bore.

loosen the exhaust pipe clip, remove the three nuts which hold the silencer (two are on the rear cross-member and the third on the front member) and remove the silencer and exhaust pipe from the machine as one unit.

It is now possible to slide the cylinder head upwards on the four long studs which secure the head and barrel to the crankcase. This done, the barrel itself can be lifted. As the piston emerges from the barrel it must be supported, and when the barrel has been placed in the box the piston should be pressed down towards the crankcase, and the mouth of the crankcase carefully blocked with rag to prevent dust and dirt entering.

There is really no need to remove the piston from the connecting rod, since it is usually possible to carry out all necessary work with the piston still in place. The first step is to examine the piston rings, which should be bright in appearance and springy to the touch. There are two rings, and if it is decided to remove them for checking in the bore it is essential that they should not be confused.

Rings are rather brittle, and care must be exercised in removing them. First, take off the top ring by easing the open ends apart, very gently, using the thumbs. The ring should be expanded just sufficiently to be lifted clear of its groove and slid over the piston towards the crown.

The lower ring should then be sprung out of its groove. It can then be slipped down the piston and off the skirt or lifted gently upwards over the top ring groove. During this operation, of course, the ends should be sprung apart slightly so that the piston is not scored. Once the ring is off

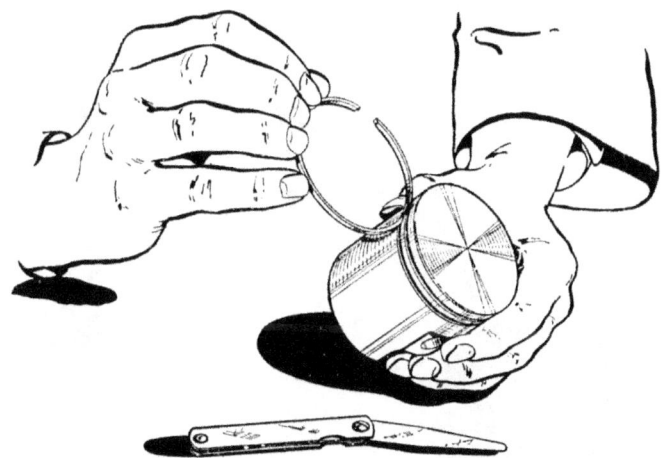

FIG. 50. CHECKING THE FIT OF THE RINGS IN THE PISTON GROOVES
The fit of the rings in the piston grooves can be checked by rolling the ring through them as illustrated.

the piston, it is an easy job to slip its open end over the connecting rod if the downward method of removal has been employed.

Any carbon on the undersides of the rings should be carefully scraped away, and if either ring is in doubtful condition—browned by burned oil or discoloured by excessive heat—it should be discarded and a new ring fitted. It is, in any case, no bad idea to have a spare set of rings handy in case of breakage.

To check the ring gap, each ring in turn is placed squarely in the cylinder bore, clear of the ports, and the gap is measured with a feeler gauge. It should be at least 0·008 in. If it is less, there is a danger of seizure when the rings expand. A very fine file can be used to cut metal away, equally, from each end of the ring. Remember that the amount to be cut is very small. If, for example, the gap measurement was 0·004 in., only 0·002 in. would need to be filed from each end of the ring to give the correct gap. Rings with excessive gaps should be discarded and replaced with new ones, which must themselves be tested for gapping in the same way.

Once satisfied that each ring is correctly gapped and free from carbon, the fit of the rings in their grooves must be checked. This is done not by refitting the ring, but by rolling it along the groove. There should be no noticeable up and down play, but the ring should roll freely. If it sticks, examine the groove. It is possible that carbon may have built up at that point. A piece of broken piston ring makes an excellent scraper for grooves, and a very fine file—such as that used for refacing contact-breaker points—can also be used to cut away high spots. It is essential, however, not to damage the groove, and if in doubt it is better to ease the

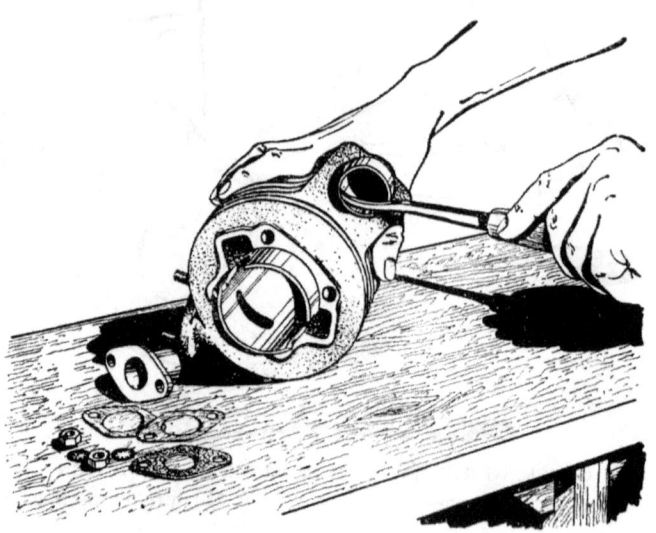

FIG. 51. CLEARING CARBON FROM THE CYLINDER PORTS WITH A SCRAPER

ring slightly. This is done by placing a piece of fine, uncreased emery cloth on a dead flat surface, and rubbing the ring over it with a rotary motion of the hand. Test it in the groove at frequent intervals—wiping the ring down with a petrol-soaked rag first to remove any emery dust—and continue the smoothing-down treatment until the ring is a correct fit.

Before refitting the rings, the carbon on the piston crown should be scraped off, taking care not to damage the light-alloy surface. Some riders like to leave a ring of carbon around the periphery of the piston, maintaining that this forms a useful pressure seal, but there is a danger here of uneven heating of the piston, and of the accumulated carbon becoming red hot and causing pre-ignition. On balance, it is better to scrape the whole of the piston crown clear of carbon, finishing off with a fine wire brush.

The sparking plug is then removed from the cylinder head, and the carbon removed from the combustion chamber. Particular care should be paid to the area around the sparking plug hole, and the threads in the hole itself should be carefully examined.

MAJOR OVERHAULS

Next, the exhaust port in the cylinder must be scraped clear of carbon, and any deposit in the transfer and inlet ports removed. In these last-named ports, however, heavy deposits are unlikely. After cleaning, the barrel should be flushed out with petrol, dried, and the working surfaces very lightly smeared with oil.

The unit can now be reassembled. The rings are fitted to the piston, great care being taken to locate the ring ends accurately against the pegs in

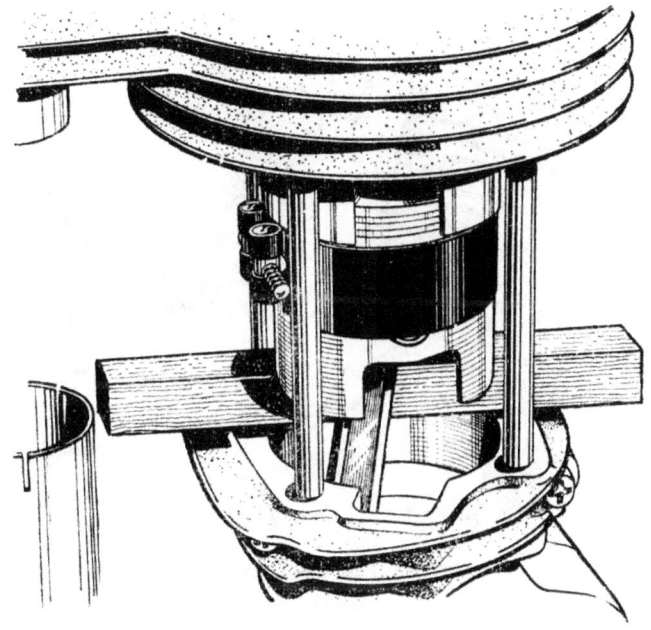

FIG. 52. REASSEMBLY

Reassembly is helped if the piston is supported from below by a wooden block and the rings are held compressed by a special tool.

the grooves, and the barrel placed on its studs. The piston is then fed into the bore, each ring in turn being compressed and gently eased into the barrel as it is lowered. They must not be forced in, or breakage will result.

When the barrel is home the head is replaced, and the nuts finger tightened. The two long extension nuts fit at the rear of the engine. When tightening them fully, take each up a couple of threads at a time, and then similarly tighten the nut diagonally opposite. After a few turns, move to the adjacent nut, then to the nut diagonally opposite from that. Proceed with this gradual tightening until they are all correctly tensioned. This seats the head properly, and avoids local stresses which might be set up if the nuts were tightened individually. Clean and re-gap the sparking plug, and refit it. Finally, lock up the crankcase pinch-bolts.

Attention can now be given to the exhaust system. Two-strokes are very fussy about their exhaust systems, and it is essential that the pipe and silencer should be free from carbon. The pipe should be detached from the silencer, and a length of bicycle chain used as a pull-through to clean out any carbon which has accumulated. The silencer tail-pipe should be examined, and any carbon poked out. If it seems that deposits are heavy,

FIG. 53. LOCKING UP THE CYLINDER CLAMPING SCREWS
This should not be done until the cylinder head nuts have been fully tightened.

it may be necessary to use a proprietary carbon-removing solution. Burning-out with an acetylene torch—a usual method—may in this case discolour the plating.

When reassembling, be careful to replace the carburettor in an absolutely vertical position, and wipe away any road dirt which has accumulated in the air trunking.

Timing the 175 c.c. Engine. Like most two-strokes, the B.S.A./Triumph 175 c.c. engine is highly sensitive to the timing of the spark—which is "fixed"—even a slight deviation from the correct setting of $\frac{5}{32}$ in. advance being sufficient to cause overheating or rough running.

To make a rough check on the timing remove the sparking plug, and insert a length of steel rod, through the plug hole, so that it bears on the piston. Grasp the flywheel, and rotate the engine gently until top dead centre is found, using the rod to "feel" the movement of the piston, and remembering that the engine runs backwards, so that the flywheel rotates anti-clockwise.

Find a convenient reference point on the engine—the top of one of the holding-down nuts, for example, and pencil a mark with a soft-lead pencil on this and a matching mark on the rod to provide a datum for top dead centre. Then make a second mark on the rod, $\frac{5}{32}$ in. *above* the t.d.c. datum. Re-insert the rod, and turn the flywheel slowly in a clockwise direction to bring this second mark into line with the mark on the engine. At this point, the contact-breaker points should just be breaking. If adjustment is required, the Phillips screws which hold the entire stator plate should be loosened slightly, and the plate turned until the points are just about to open. Then tighten the screws, and recheck the timing. Turning the plate clockwise advances the timing; turning it anti-clockwise will retard it. Inaccuracies in gapping the points also affect the timing. The correct gap, when fully open, is 0·020 in. Widening the gap advances the timing, closing it retards. It is essential, therefore, to check the contact-breaker gap before altering the timing, and to test the effect of adjustment if an error is found. After retiming, too, the gap must be checked and adjusted if necessary, and the timing finally rechecked when this has been done.

The 175 c.c. Clutch. Providing you possess the necessary clutch extractor (Tool No. 61-5007) it is possible to change the clutch plates without a great deal of dismantling. First, of course, the valance must be removed from the left-hand side of the machine, and the area around the primary chaincase cleaned with degreasing fluid hosed off with water. The parts are then dried before dismantling commences. The rear end of the machine is then lifted clear of the ground by blocking-up with wood under the rear cross-member, and the rear wheel is removed. The curved, light-alloy support arm must be taken off the chaincase. It is located by three bolts, and in addition there is a centre bolt which secures the bearing cap. This, too, must be removed, and the arm slid off the bearing. The plain steel bush on the bearing spindle, together with its thrust washer, must be taken off. After disconnecting the cable from the clutch operating arm the eight Phillips screws and single $\frac{5}{16}$ in. nut and bolt which hold the primary casing must be removed.

By tapping the case with a rawhide mallet, or a block of softwood, the joint can now be broken. A baking tin should have been placed beneath the unit, since the oil in the case will drain out once the cover is lifted away. The clutch-operating mechanism will come away with the case.

Using a forked screwdriver, remove the three nuts holding the clutch springs. Each nut should be released by only a couple of turns at a time. With these removed, the nuts, plate and springs can be taken off and placed to one side.

Removal of the plate reveals a large nut, which is locked by a tab washer.

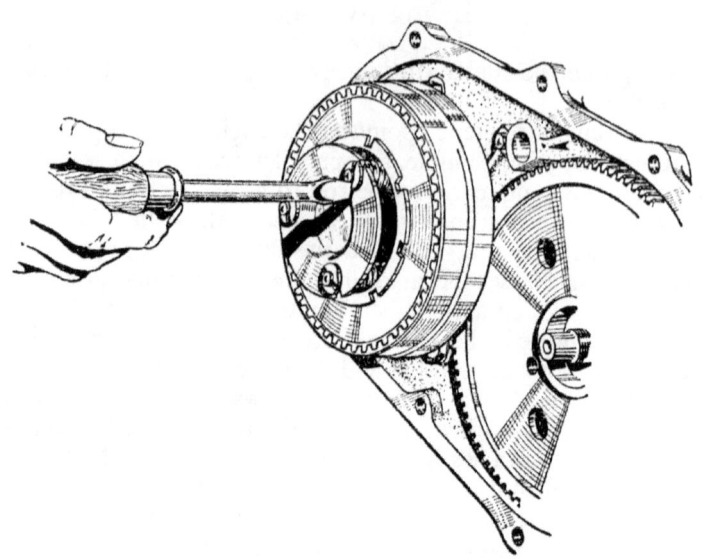

Fig. 54. Removal of the Primary Chain Case
After this the clutch spring can be undone.

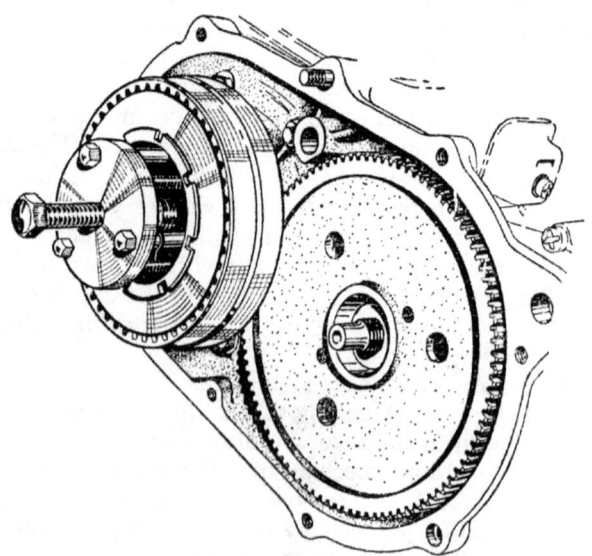

Fig. 55. Removal of the Clutch Centre
This can only be done with the correct extractor.

This must be flattened, the transmission locked by placing the machine in gear and applying the rear brake, and the nut undone. This job requires care, since it is easy to damage the clutch spring studs if the spanner slips. Once the nut and tab washer have been removed, the clutch centre extractor is fitted, and the centre and plates drawn off, leaving the housing, distance-piece and bearing in position.

When reassembling, one of the steel plates is placed on the clutch centre, followed by a bonded plate, and then another steel plate, alternating

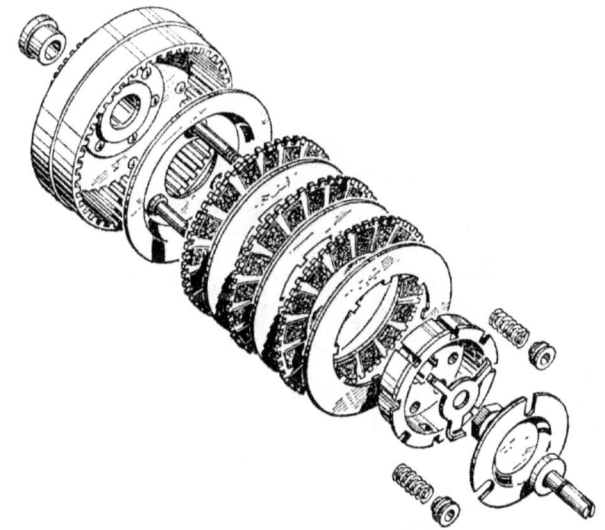

FIG. 56. AN EXPLODED VIEW OF THE CLUTCH
Exposed to view are the clutch centre and tab washer and the driving and driven plates.

between the two until all the plates are fitted. Line up the splines of the driven plates, temporarily fit the spring plate with a single spring and nut to hold the assembly together, and slide it into the clutch body. Once it is home, remove the spring plate again, fit a new tab washer, tighten the nut, and peen the washer over to lock it.

The three springs are now replaced, the spring plate fitted, and the three nuts tightened evenly until the spring plate sits squarely, exactly $\frac{3}{16}$ in. from the clutch centre flange at all points.

Clean any oil away from the mating faces of the two parts of the primary case, using a rag soaked in petrol, and apply jointing compound to both. Place a new gasket in position on the case, press the joint cleanly together, and replace the eight screws and the front nut and bolt. Finally, reconnect the clutch cable, replace the support arm and rear wheel, and fill the case with oil to the correct level. After fitting new plates, it will be necessary to readjust the clutch control cable, and a further adjustment will have to be made once the plates have settled, after a few hundred miles running.

DECARBONIZING THE 250 c.c. ENGINE

Unlike the two-stroke, in which some of the oil mixed with the petrol is necessarily burned during running, the 250 c.c. four-stroke is less likely to collect a heavy carbon deposit, and the real object of stripping the head from this unit is not to remove the carbon, but to examine and renovate

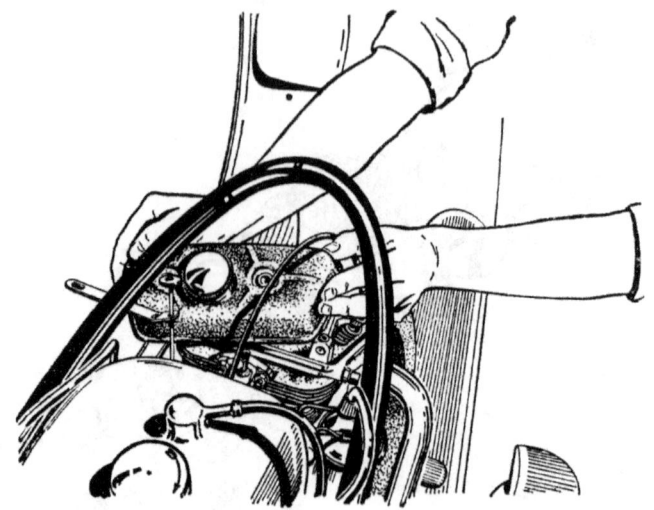

FIG. 57. DECARBONIZING THE 250 C.C. ENGINE
First remove the side valances and air trunking, and then take off the rocker box cover.

the valves and their seatings, upon which the efficiency of the cylinder sealing depends.

To carry out a normal top overhaul—as this form of work is more accurately called—it is not necessary to remove the engine unit from the frame, but the side valances will have to be taken off to give access to the unit.

Besides the normal tool kit, it is essential to have a few special items—a valve spring compressor (Tool No. 61-5001); a suction-type valve grinding tool (Tool No. 61-5035); and scrapers, either professional, or home-made by filing down a stick of solder or a piece of softwood to wedge shape. A top overhaul gasket set (No. 00-3120) will be necessary, and if the condition of the valves is suspect a set of spare valves and springs should also be obtained. For the actual work of seating the valves, a tin of coarse and a tin of fine grinding paste will be wanted; and you should also have a supply of fresh engine oil.

MAJOR OVERHAULS

Once the side valances have been removed, the next step is to detach the sparking plug leads.

If, when the cowling is removed, the engine unit proves to be dirty, it is advisable to brush it over with degreasing fluid, and hose it down gently to remove the dirt. It must subsequently be dried with clean rag before the work continues.

When removing the carburettor, do not interfere with the joint between the instrument and its stub. Instead, remove the two nuts which hold the actual inlet manifold to the cylinder head, and take off the carburettor

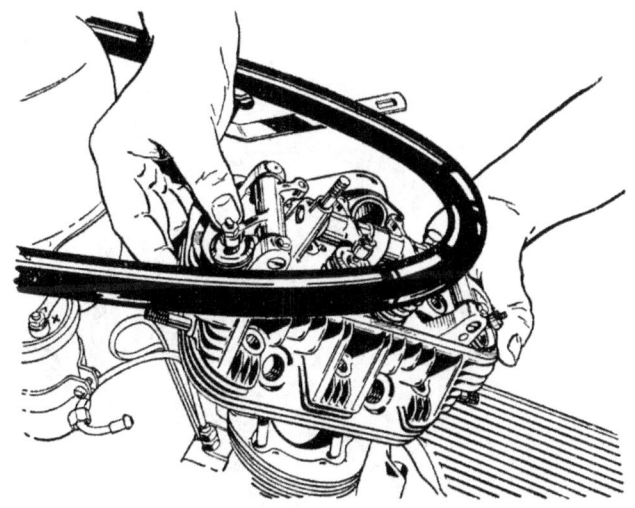

FIG. 58. REMOVAL OF THE CYLINDER HEAD
The cylinder head is turned and slightly inclined to lift it away from the machine

with the manifold still attached to it. Then release the nuts which hold the exhaust pipe, and pull the pipe away from its studs.

Undo the rocker cover nuts—one holds the petrol tap support bracket—and lift the rocker cover away to gain access to the head nuts. Slacken the lower unions of the oil pipes, and completely undo the upper unions. The pipes can then be swivelled out of the way. The sparking plugs and the seven cylinder head nuts should next be removed, and so should the left-hand rocker stud, which is equipped with a hexagon for this purpose. A sharp tug will now free the cylinder head, complete with the push rods. The joint face gasket between the head and the barrels may also come away. Even if it appears to be sound, it should be scrapped, and a new gasket fitted when reassembly commences.

Place the head out of harm's way temporarily, and bring the pistons to the top of the stroke. Use a scraper to remove all carbon from the two piston crowns, taking care not to allow it to dig into the soft metal. Blow the carbon dust away, using a tyre pump, and then lower the pistons an inch or so and carefully wipe any carbon away from the top of the bores.

Cover the cylinder bores with plugs of clean, non-fluffy rag, and turn your attention to the cylinder head. The condition of the valve seats can be checked by pressing on each valve stem in turn, and examining the valves themselves and their seats. In all probability, the seats will be discoloured, or have a slightly speckled appearance caused by pitting of the metal. If so, the next step is to remove the valves. The valve spring compressor is fitted into place, and the screw operated to compress the

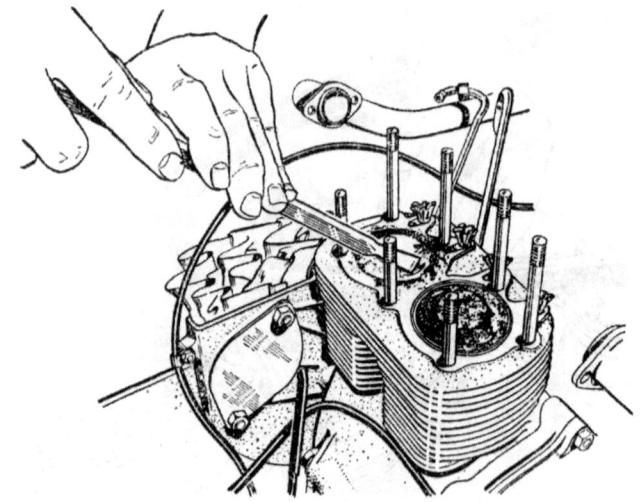

Fig. 59. Carbon on the Piston Crowns is Scraped Away Without Disturbing the Pistons

valve springs. As this is done, the two small split collets which lock the springs to the valve can be lifted out of place, and the valve tool is then unscrewed to free the valve and springs. Each valve, as it is removed, should be marked to show its position, and then placed in a box with its collets and end cap.

When all the valves have been removed, the carbon deposit is cleaned from the head, using a scraper. The final burnishing can be given by a wire brush fitted to a rotary drill. Attention should be paid to the threads of the sparking plug holes, since carbon is apt to collect in the lower threads. It should be eased out of these very carefully.

Any carbon in the ports should also be removed, and here a wire brush, used with a flexible extension from an electric drill, is an excellent tool for giving the final polish. However, in all this work on the head you must be very careful not to damage the faces which mate with the cylinder barrel.

After the work on the head is complete, the valves must also be scraped clean. Carbon on the valve stems can be scraped off, and the finishing touches made by polishing with a narrow strip of emery cloth wound round the stem and tugged backwards and forwards while the valve is

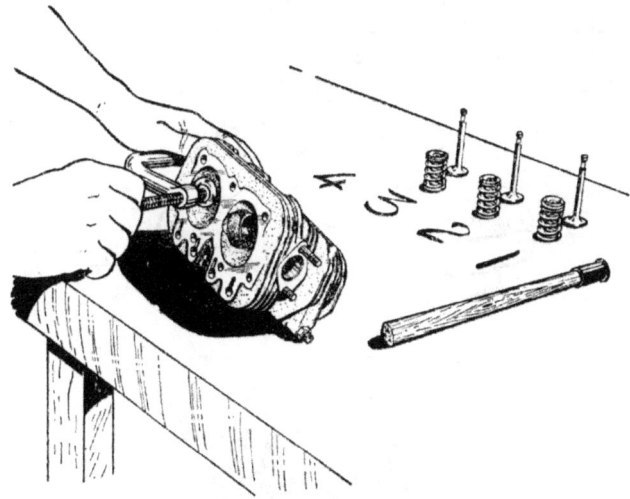

Fig. 60. Removal of the Valves
A valve spring compressor is used to remove the valves which are placed with their springs, collars and collets in order on the bench.

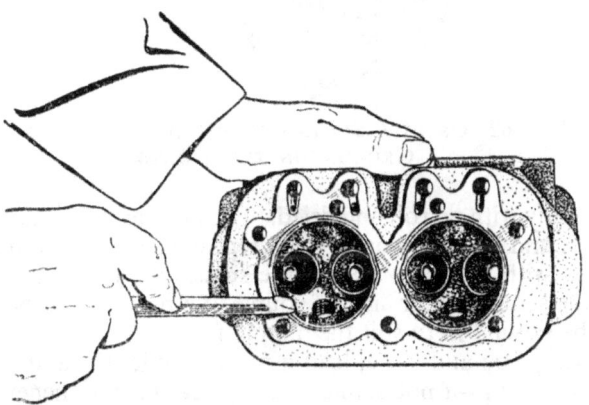

Fig. 61. Scraping Deposits Away From the Combustion Chambers
Care should be taken not to damage the mating faces of the cylinder head joint.

securely held. Immediately afterwards, wash the valve stem thoroughly in clean petrol.

To grind in a valve, coarse grinding paste is spread thinly on the seating face and the valve is then slipped back into its guide. The rubber suction tool is applied to the valve head.

With the valve lightly pressed into place, the tool is oscillated rapidly by rubbing the handle between one's hands. After half a dozen such movements the valve is lifted, and turned a quarter of a turn. It is then once again pressed into place on the seat, another half a dozen oscillations made, and the process repeated. Grinding should not be overdone, and it should cease as soon as the valve and head faces both show a continuous line of matt silver-grey. At this stage, the valve is removed, the two faces

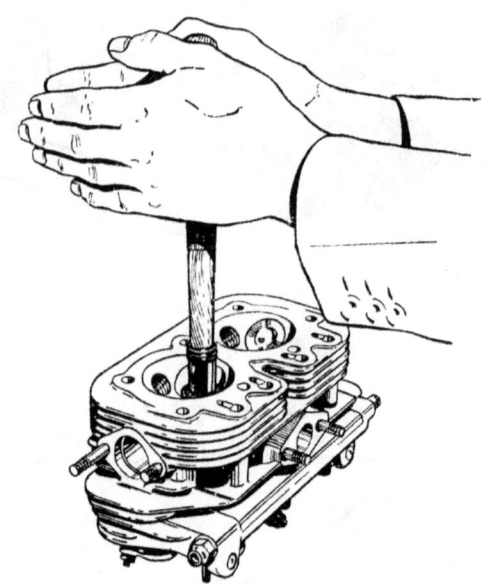

FIG. 62. USING A SUCTION-TYPE VALVE TOOL FOR GRINDING-IN THE VALVES

washed liberally with petrol, and dried. Then fine grinding paste is applied to the valve, and the grinding process repeated to give the final seal. A second wash with petrol completes the sequence. Each valve should be treated in the same manner and, of course, if a new valve is being fitted it, too, must be ground in to suit the mating face.

Valve springs, by and large, lead a pretty hectic life, and it is usual at least to check them—if not actually to replace them—whenever the head is removed. If you have a vice in the workshop you can make a quite satisfactory check by placing in its jaws one of the old valve springs and one of the new ones, butted against a small metal spacer placed between them. Tighten the jaws of the vice until the springs are roughly the length which they adopt when fitted to the head, and measure each spring. If the lengths are the same replacement is unnecessary, but if the used spring has shortened by more than 5 per cent. compared with the new spring it is better to use new parts.

Occasionally, it may be desirable to replace the valve guides. If, when the valve is slipped into the guide, it is possible to rock the valve stem to and fro it indicates that the guide is worn. Using a special tool (No. 61–3382) from the combustion chamber side, the old guide can be driven out, and the same tool is used to drive in a new guide, working, this time, from the rocker-box side of the head.

To reassemble the valve gear, each valve in turn is slipped into its guide,

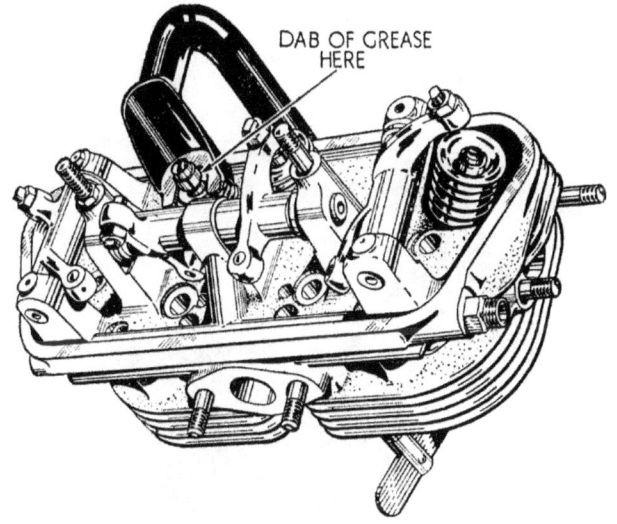

FIG. 63. WHEN REPLACING THE VALVES, A DAB OF GREASE APPLIED TO THE VALVE NECK WILL HOLD THE COLLETS WHILE THE SPRING IS REFITTED

its spring and collar placed loosely over the stem, and the valve spring compressor used to compress the spring sufficiently to allow the collets to be inserted. If a dab of grease is applied to each collet before assembly it will help to hold them in position while the compressor is released. This should be done gently at first, watching the while to check that the collets take up position properly in the collar. Then the tool is freed, and the next valve inserted.

Grease comes in handy when replacing the head, too. A dab is placed in the cup of each valve rocker, and the end of the push-rod pressed into it. This is sufficient to hold the push-rods in place while the head is being eased into position over its holding studs. Don't forget, however, to fit the new jointing gasket first. No jointing compound should be used, but both faces of the gasket should be lightly smeared with oil. Before refitting the head, it is advisable to slacken the adjuster screws on the rockers, or the push-rods may be bent when the head is locked down.

As soon as the head is properly seated, the plain steel washers should be replaced on the cylinder head studs, and the nuts tightened with the fingers. Then each nut is tightened, with a spanner, by about half a turn at a time, working in a definite sequence. First, turn the nut which is located between the sparking plugs. The nut behind No. 3 valve follows; then the nut behind No. 2 valve. Next the left-hand nut on the front of the head is turned, followed by the equivalent right-hand nut. Next comes the nut behind No. 4 valve, and finally the nut behind No. 1 valve. This completes the sequence, which is then repeated until all the nuts are tight.

Now the carburettor and the exhaust pipes can be refitted, followed by the cylinder head air ducting. This done, the tappets have to be reset to

FIG. 64. REPLACING THE HEAD
The head is replaced complete with its push rods which are held in place by grease applied to the rocker cups.

0·005 in., using the routine described in Chapter 7. Clean, gap and refit the sparking plugs; replace the rocker cover and connect the oil pipes, and the mechanical work is done.

It is important to remember, however, that valve grinding, as described here, is only effective where pitting on the valve seats or the valve itself is of a minor character. Really heavy pitting cannot be dealt with in this way, and the valve seats will need to be recut to an angle of 45°. This can only be done with a valve-cutting tool, and it is a job which calls for considerable skill if damage is not to be done. Where the initial inspection of the valves shows that deep pitting has occurred, it is better to take the head and valves to an approved B.S.A. or Triumph dealer and get him to recut the seats in his workshop.

Piston removal should rarely be necessary, but if the engine has been

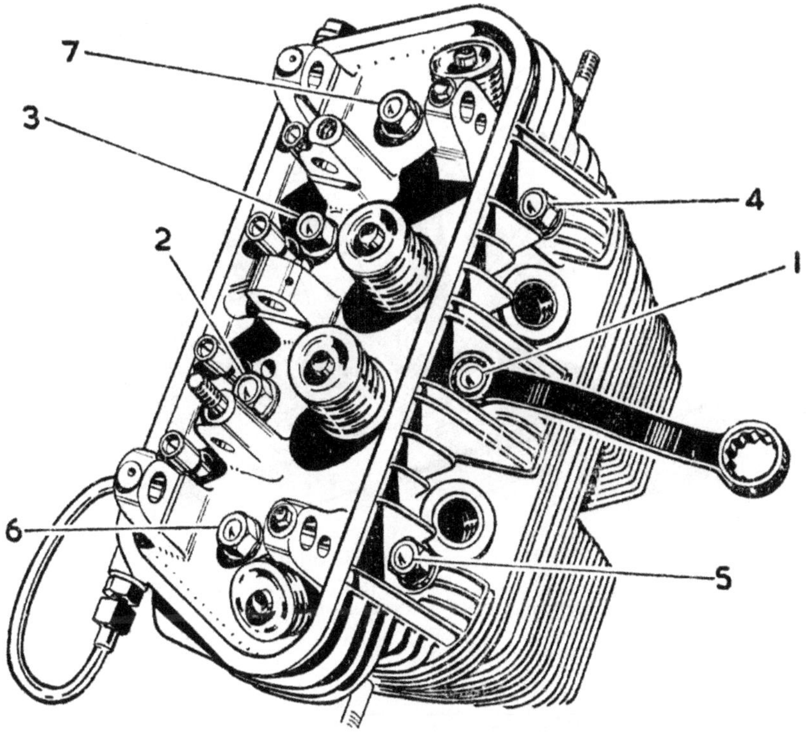

Fig. 65. When tightening the Head Bolts it is Essential to Follow the Sequence Shown in this Drawing

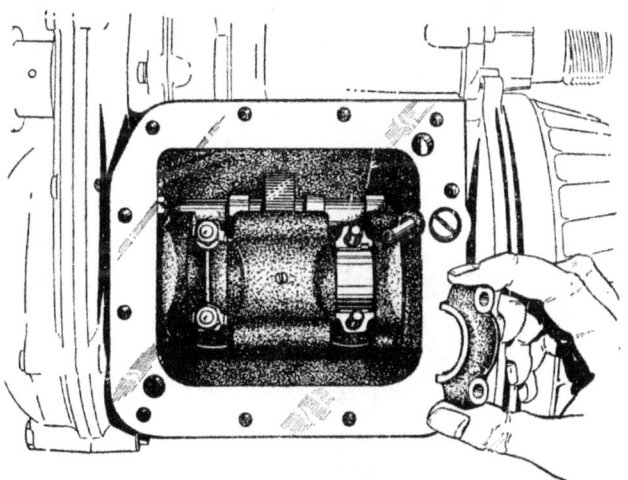

Fig. 66. The Big-end Bearings can be Inspected by Draining and Removing the Sump

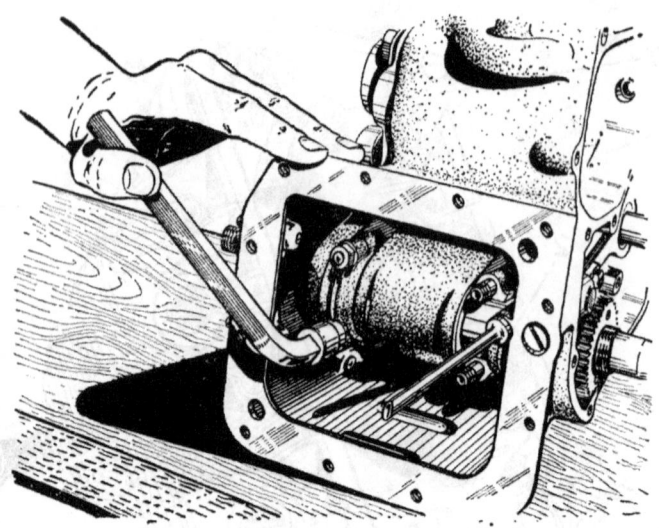

FIG. 67. REPLACING THE BEARING END CAPS

A torque wrench should be used but if this is not available tighten the nuts carefully and evenly without straining the threads.

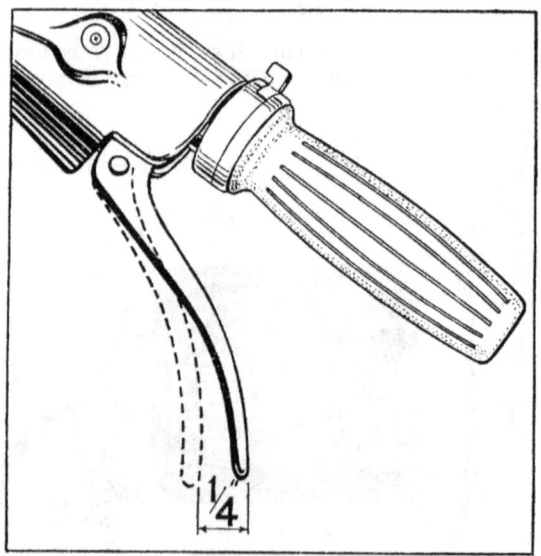

FIG. 68. ADJUSTING THE CLUTCH

It is essential that the clutch is kept in correct adjustment giving a quarter of an inch of play in the cable, measured at the end of the lever. This prevents clutch slip. More play may cause the clutch to drag.

MAJOR OVERHAULS 103

seized for any reason it is possible that the rings may have been broken, and the engine must never be run in this condition.

The procedure is much the same as for decarbonizing, save that the oil must be drained from the sump. When the head is off, the machine is laid on its side or raised on blocks or trestles, and the sump is removed.

Turn the engine over until the pistons are at the bottom of the stroke, remove the bolts, nuts and washers which secure the end caps of the big-end bearing. A gentle upwards tap with a block of wood and a hammer will free the caps, which can then be lifted out. Gently turn the engine to take the pistons to the top of the bore, when a gentle push on the connecting rods will lift them clear of the barrel, complete with the rods. The only circumstance in which this procedure is impossible is if excessive engine wear has resulted in the formation of ridges at the top of the bores, when the engine unit will have to be completely stripped.

When reassembling, it is important to note that the big-end bolts must be tightened with a torque wrench, and that this must be set to a reading of 140–180 lb-in.

The 250 c.c. Clutch. Generally speaking, the dismantling procedure for the clutch on the twin-cylinder machines is the same as that for the single-cylinder model described on pages 91–94. The side valances must be removed, and the curved support arm disconnected after blocking up the machine and removing the rear wheel. Then, the left-hand rear engine mounting bolt must be removed and the oil drained from the primary case. Once the screws and the two nuts holding the primary cover have been taken off, the low-tension leads from the distributor to the h.t. coils must be unscrewed at the coil ends, and the oil-feed pipe on the cover must also be disconnected.

Thereafter, for both dismantling and reassembly of the clutch the procedure is exactly the same as that for the smaller machine.

Timing the 250 c.c. Engine. To obtain the best performance from the ignition system of the twin-cylinder machine it is essential that the timing is such that the spark, fully retarded, occurs 5° before top dead centre. This is the setting given to each machine before it leaves the factory, and it is most unlikely that it will be altered accidentally. If, however, the timing is "lost" for any reason it is essential to reset it as accurately as possible. The timing may also be affected slightly after re-adjustment of the contact-breaker points.

To check the timing, remove the rocker cover and the sparking plugs. Insert a length of rod through the nearside plug hole, and bring the piston in that cylinder to t.d.c. making sure that both valves are closed. If one is open, the piston is on the exhaust stroke!

Now engage gear and, by turning the rear wheel, move the engine backwards by 45°—one-eighth of a turn. Remove the cover of the

Fig. 69. Draining the Primary Drive
The level plug is removed and the scooter tilted to the left.

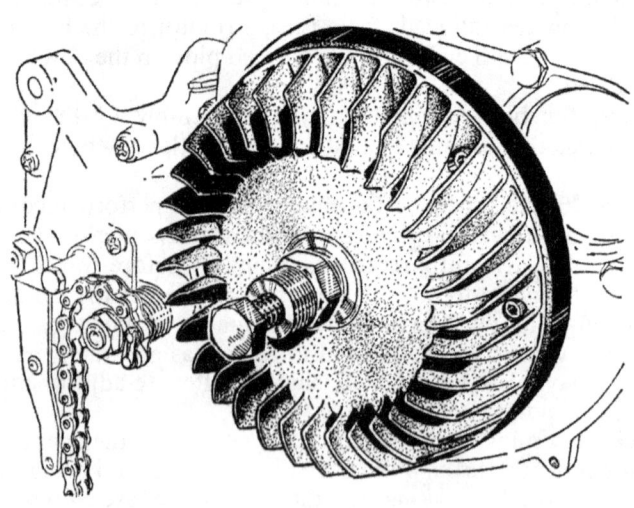

Fig. 70. Removal of the Flywheel
This should rarely be necessary but it is an easy task providing the correct extractor (No. 61–5002) is used.

contact-breaker, and watch the uppermost set of points as the wheel is again turned forwards to bring the piston back towards top dead centre.

As soon as the points begin to open, stop turning the wheel. A double check can be made by inserting a cigarette paper between the points, which will grip it until they are just on the point of opening, when the paper can be withdrawn with a gentle pull.

At this point, the piston should be within 5° of t.d.c. This can be checked easily with a degree plate fitted to the flywheel, or by observing the position of the vanes on the flywheel itself. As these are set 11° apart, five degrees is equivalent to roughly half the distance between two vanes, so if a line taken vertically from the crankshaft centre falls midway between two vanes the setting is correct.

If the points are either open too wide, or are still closed at the 5° retarded position, slacken the two hexagons which hold the contact-breaker backplate, and turn the plate until the desired points setting is achieved. Lock the plate in this position, and recheck the settings before replacing the rocker cover and the plugs.

Fuel Starvation on the 250 c.c. Machine. On some machines, an air lock tends to form in the fuel pipe when the fuel level in the tank is becoming low. To cure this, switch off the petrol, and undo the banjo union on the carburettor, taking care not to lose the inner fibre washer as the union is removed.

Re-route the fuel pipe so that it runs beneath the clamping screw of the carburettor, and then curls upwards, over the screw, to the float chamber. In this position, the fuel pipe is almost vertical at the union. Hold the inner fibre washer in position with one finger while the union is being tightened.

Checking the 250 c.c. Scooter Starter Motor. The only general maintenance necessary with the Lucas M3 pre-engaged starter motor fitted to the self-starter models is to keep the supply terminal on the starter switch clean and tight; to clean the connexion if it has become dirty; and to smear the contacting surfaces lightly with petroleum jelly.

To test the starter motor without removing it from the machine, switch on the headlamp and operate the starter. If the lamp dims, but the starter fails to crank the engine, remove the sparking plug and check that the engine is not abnormally stiff. Providing no fault is found the sparking plugs should be replaced, and a substitute battery tried.

Should there be no dimming of the headlamp when the starter is operated and the motor does not turn, the tightness of the starter switch terminal connexion should be checked. Any further checking requires the use of bench equipment, and should be referred to an approved B.S.A. or Triumph dealer.

CHAPTER IX

FOR READY REFERENCE

175 c.c. *Engine.* Two-stroke; 61·5 mm bore × 58 mm stroke = 173 c.c.
Compression ratio, 7:1.
Petroil ratio, 1 in 20 (standard oils) 1 in 16 (self-mixing oils).
Ignition timing, $\frac{5}{32}$ before t.d.c.
Plug gap, 0·025 in.
Plug, Champion L 5.
Contact-breaker gap, 0·020 in.
Carburettor, Amal 363/11.
Main jet, 130.
Pilot jet, 15.
Needle jet, 106.
Needle jet position, 3.
Throttle slide, 363/2½.
Main bearings, ball $\frac{3}{4}$ in. × $1\frac{7}{8}$ in. × $\frac{9}{16}$ in., drive side and timing side, deep groove.
Ball 17 × 40 × 12 mm drive side and timing side, deep groove.
Big-end bearing, roller, 4 × 8 mm on $\frac{15}{32}$ in.-diameter pin. 18 rollers.
Piston ring gap, 0·013 in. maximum.

175 c.c. *Gearbox and Transmission.* Gearbox, four-speed, positive-stop foot control, with neutral selector.
Primary drive, 2·27:1 reduction; crankshaft gear 45 T; secondary gear 102 T.
Secondary drive, Duplex chain, 94 links × 0·375 in. pitch.
Overall ratios, top, 4·93:1; 3rd, 6·29:1; 2nd, 10·08:1; 1st, 14·75:1
Clutch, engine-speed type; three springs, 105 lb pressure.

250 c.c. *Engine.* Vertical twin four-stroke; 56 mm bore × 50·62 mm stroke = 249 c.c.
Compression ratio, 6·5:1.
Ignition timing, 5° before t.d.c. at full retard.

Valve timing, inlet opens 10° before t.d.c. closes 50° after b.d.c.
exhaust opens 50° before b.d.c., closes 10° after t.d.c.
Plug gap, 0·025 in.
Plug, Champion L7/JA/548.
Contact-breaker gap, 0·015 in.
Tappet clearance, 0·005 in. inlet and exhaust, with engine cold.
Carburettor, Zenith 17 MXZ.
Main jet, 82.
Pilot jet, 45.
Needle jet, fixed.
Needle jet position, fixed.
Starter slide, 200.
Main bearings, ball 25 × 62, 15 mm deep groove drive side; plain $1\frac{1}{8}$ in. diameter × $\frac{7}{8}$ in. wide, timing side.
Big-end bearing, plain, $1\frac{1}{8}$ in. diameter (crankpin).
Piston ring gap, 0·013 in. maximum.
Valve springs, double springs, closed load 45 lb, open load $67\frac{1}{2}$ lb.
Valve spring free length, $1\frac{9}{16}$ in. (outer); $1\frac{1}{2}$ in. approx. (inner).

250 c.c. *Gearbox and Transmission.* Gearbox, four-speed, positive-stop, foot control, with neutral selector.
Primary drive, 2:1 reduction; crankshaft gear 49 T; secondary gear 98 T.
Overall ratios, top, 4:1; 3rd, 5·2:1; 2nd, 8:1; 1st, 12:1.
Clutch, engine-speed type, three springs, 105 lb pressure.

Both models. Tyre size, 3·50 in. × 10 in.
Tyre pressures, 17 lb sq in. front; 24 lb sq in. rear (solo); or 30 lb sq in. (with passenger).
Brakes, internal-expanding, 5 in. dia. × 1 in. width.
Steering head angle, 65°.
Steering lock angle, 45°.
Trail, $3\frac{3}{4}$ in.
Front fork movement, $4\frac{3}{8}$ in.
Rear suspension movement, $2\frac{19}{32}$ in.
Wheelbase, 48 in.
Width, 24 in.
Ground clearance, 5 in.
Fuel tank, $1\frac{1}{2}$ gal. capacity.
Sump capacity (250 c.c. only), $2\frac{1}{2}$ pints.
Weight, 175 c.c., 236 lb dry; 250 c.c., 244 lb dry.

NOTES

INDEX

AIR, 6, 11
Air filter, 13
Amal carburettor, 74-6, 106

BATTERY, 37, 41, 70
Big end, 6, 101, 102, 106, 107
Bodywork, 55, 56, 57
Brake—
 adjustment, 82
 removal, 48-50
Brakes, general, 18, 26, 27, 28, 81, 82, 107
Bulbs, 37, 41

CABLES, 18, 62, 77
Carburettor, *see also* Amal and Zenith, 11-13, 32, 33
Chain adjustment, 80, 82
Clutch, 16, 24, 76-8, 91, 92, 93
 adjustment (both models), 76, 77, 78, 102, 103
Compression ratio, 6, 106
Connecting rod, 6, 102, 103
Contact breaker, 14, 15, 69, 70
Controls, 20, 21, 25
Cornering, 28, 29
Crankpin, 5
Crankshaft, 5, 106
Cylinder, 5, 85, 86, 89
Cylinder head, 5, 85, 100, 101

DAILY maintenance, 61
Dashboard 57
Decarbonizing (250 c.c.), 94-103
Decarbonizing (175 c.c.), 84-90

ELECTRICAL circuits—
 (250 c.c.), 38, 39
 (175 c.c.), 40
Engine—
 principles, 5-11
 types, 2, 4

FAULT tracing, 32-41
Flywheel magneto, 34

Frame, 45
Front forks, 17, 45, 46, 47, 50, 52, 53
Fuel, 6
 petroil, 106
 starvation, 105

GEARBOX, 16, 62, 76, 79, 106
Gear changing, 21, 22, 26
Gear ratios, 106
Generator, A.C., 69, 104
Gudgeon pin, 6

HANDLEBAR controls, 20, 21, 22
Handlebars, 46, 50, 58
Headlamp, 35
Hydraulic dampers, 18, 53, 54

IGNITION—
 coil, 35
 leads, 35
 timing, 90, 91, 103, 104, 106

JETS, 106, 107

KICK STARTER, 21, 25

LIGHTING sets, 37
Lubrication, 36, 65, 64, 65, 104

MAINTENANCE, routine, 60-82

NEUTRAL selector, 22, 80

PETROIL, 10, 11
Petrol tap, 32, 33
Piston 5, 6, 7, 8, 9, 86, 87, 88, 89
 rings, 87, 88, 89

SELF-starter, 105
Sidecars, 29-31
Silencer, 86, 90
Sparking plugs, 33, 63, 68, 106, 107
Specifications, 106, 107
Speedometer, 23
Steering head, 46

Suspension systems, 2
Switches, 23, 24

TAPPETS, 36, 66, 67, 68
Tools, 42–44
Transmission, 15–17, 64
Twist grip, 25, 48
Tyre pressures, 63, 107

VALVE grinding, 97, 98

Valve springs, 5, 96, 98, 99
Valve timing, 107
Valves, 5

WEEKLY maintenance, 61
Weights, 107
Wiring diagram (250 c.c.), 38, 39
Wiring diagram (175 c.c.), 40

ZENITH carburettor, 72, 73, 75, 107

VELOCEPRESS MANUALS – MOTORCYCLE BY MAKE

AJS 1932-1948 SINGLES & TWINS 250cc THRU 1000cc (BOOK OF)
AJS 1945-1960 SINGLES 350cc & 500cc MODELS 16 & 18 (BOOK OF)
AJS 1955-1965 SINGLES 350cc & 500cc (BOOK OF)
ARIEL UP TO 1932 (BOOK OF)
ARIEL 1932-1939 PREWAR MODELS (BOOK OF)
ARIEL 1933-1951 (WORKSHOP MANUAL)
ARIEL 1939-1960 4 STROKE SINGLES (BOOK OF)
ARIEL 1958-1964 LEADER & ARROW (BOOK OF)
BMW R26 R27 (1956-1967) FACTORY WORKSHOP MANUAL
BMW R50 R50S R60 R69S (1955-1969) FACTORY WORKSHOP MANUAL
BRIDGESTONE 90 SERIES FACTORY WSM & PARTS CATALOGUE
BRIDGESTONE 175 SERIES FACTORY WSM & PARTS CATALOGUE
BRIDGESTONE 350 SERIES FACTORY WSM & PARTS CATALOGUES
BSA SUNBEAM SCOOTER WORKSHOP MANUAL 1959-1965
BSA SUNBEAM SCOOTER (BOOK OF)
BSA SERVICE SHEETS MASTER CATALOGUE ALL MODELS 1945-1967
BSA BANTAM D1 TO D7 1948-1966 FACTORY SERVICE SHEETS MANUAL
BSA BANTAM ALL MODELS FROM 1948 ONWARDS (BOOK OF)
BSA SINGLES & V-TWINS UP TO 1927 (BOOK OF)
BSA SINGLES & V-TWINS UP TO 1930 (BOOK OF)
BSA SINGLES & V-TWINS UP TO 1935 (BOOK OF)
BSA SINGLES & V-TWINS 1936-1939 (BOOK OF)
BSA C10, C11 & C12 1945-1958 FACTORY SERVICE SHEETS MANUAL
BSA OHV & SV SINGLES 250-600cc 1945-1959 (BOOK OF)
BSA C15 & B40 1958-1967 FACTORY SERVICE SHEETS MANUAL
BSA OHV & SV SINGLES 250cc (ONLY) 1954-1970 (BOOK OF)
BSA B31, B32, B33 & B34 1945-60 FACTORY SERVICE SHEETS MANUAL
BSA OHV SINGLES 350 & 500cc 1955-1967 (BOOK OF)
BSA M20, M21 & M33 1945-1963 FACTORY SERVICE SHEETS MANUAL
BSA TWINS A7 & A10 1948-1962 FACTORY SERVICE SHEETS MANUAL
BSA TWINS A7 & A10 1948-1962 (BOOK OF)
BSA TWINS A50 & A65 1962-1965 FACTORY WORKSHOP MANUAL
BSA TWINS A50 & A65 1962-1969 (SECOND BOOK OF)
DOUGLAS 1929-1939 PREWAR ALL MODELS (BOOK OF)
DOUGLAS 1948-1957 POSTWAR ALL MODELS FACTORY SHOP MANUAL
DUCATI 160cc, 250cc & 350cc OHC MODELS FACTORY SHOP MANUAL
HONDA 50 ALL MODELS UP TO 1970 INC MONKEY & TRAIL (BOOK OF)
HONDA 90 ALL MODELS UP TO 1966 (BOOK OF)
HONDA 125-150cc TWINS C/CS/CB/CA FACTORY WORKSHOP MANUAL
HONDA 250-305 TWINS C/CS/CB FACTORY WORKSHOP MANUAL
HONDA 450 CB/CL 1965-1974 K0 TO K7 FACTORY WORKSHOP MANUAL
HONDA C100 SUPER CUB FACTORY WORKSHOP MANUAL
HONDA C110 SPORT CUB 1962-1969 FACTORY WORKSHOP MANUAL
HONDA TWINS & SINGLES 50cc THRU 305cc 1960-1966 (BOOK OF)
HONDA TWINS ALL MODELS 125cc THRU 450cc UP TO 1968 (BOOK OF)
INDIAN PONYBIKE, BOY RACER & PAPOOSE ILL PARTS LIST & SALES LIT
J.A.P. ENGINES 1927-1952 & MOTORCYCLES 1934-1952 (BOOK OF)
LAMBRETTA 1947-1957 ALL 125 & 150cc MODELS (BOOK OF)
LAMBRETTA 1957-1970 LI & TV MODELS (SECOND BOOK OF)
MATCHLESS 1931-1939 ALL MODELS 250cc THRU 990cc (BOOK OF)
MATCHLESS 1945-1956 350 & 500cc SINGLES (BOOK OF)
MATCHLESS 1955-1966 350 & 500cc SINGLES (BOOK OF)
NEW IMPERIAL ALL SV & OHV FROM 1935 ONWARDS (BOOK OF)
NORTON 1932-1939 PREWAR MODELS (BOOK OF)
NORTON 1932-1947 (BOOK OF)
NORTON 1938-1956 (BOOK OF)
NORTON 1955-1963 MODELS 19, 50 & ES2 (BOOK OF)
NORTON 1955-1965 DOMINATOR TWINS (BOOK OF)
NORTON 1960-1970 TWIN CYLINDER FACTORY WORKSHOP MANUAL
NORTON 1970-1975 COMMANDO FACTORY WORKSHOP MANUAL
NORTON 1975-1978 MK 3 COMMANDO FACTORY WORKSHOP MANUAL
NSU PRIMA 1956-1964 ALL MODELS (BOOK OF)
NSU QUICKLY 1953-1963 ALL MODELS (BOOK OF)
PANTHER 1932-1958 LIGHTWEIGHT MODELS 250 & 350cc (BOOK OF)
PANTHER 1938-1966 HEAVYWEIGHT MODELS 600 & 650cc (BOOK OF)
RALEIGH MOPEDS 1960-1969 (BOOK OF)
RALEIGH MOTORCYCLES 1919-1933 (BOOK OF)
ROYAL ENFIELD 1934-1946 SINGLES & V TWINS (BOOK OF)
ROYAL ENFIELD 1937-1953 SINGLES & V TWINS (BOOK OF)
ROYAL ENFIELD 1946-1962 SINGLES (BOOK OF)
ROYAL ENFIELD 1958-1966 250cc & 350cc SINGLES (SECOND BOOK OF)
ROYAL ENFIELD 736cc INTERCEPTOR FACTORY WORKSHOP MANUAL
RUDGE 1933-1939 (BOOK OF)
SUNBEAM 1928-1939 (BOOK OF)
SUNBEAM 1946-1957 S7 & S8 (BOOK OF)
SUZUKI 50cc & 80cc UP TO 1966 (BOOK OF)
SUZUKI T10 1963-1967 FACTORY WORKSHOP MANUAL
SUZUKI T20 & T200 1965-1969 FACTORY WORKSHOP MANUAL
SUZUKI TWINS 1962 ONWARDS 125-500cc WORKSHOP MANUAL
TRIUMPH TIGRESS SCOOTER WORKSHOP MANUAL 1959-1965
TRIUMPH TIGRESS SCOOTER (BOOK OF)
TRIUMPH 1935-1939 PREWAR MODELS (BOOK OF)
TRIUMPH 1935-1949 (BOOK OF)
TRIUMPH 1937-1951 (WORKSHOP MANUAL)
TRIUMPH 1945-1955 FACTORY WORKSHOP MANUAL
TRIUMPH 1945-1958 TWINS (BOOK OF)
TRIUMPH 1956-1969 TWINS (BOOK OF)
VELOCETTE 1925-1970 ALL SINGLES & TWINS (BOOK OF)
VESPA 1951-1961 (BOOK OF)
VESPA 1955-1963 125 & 150cc & GS MODELS (SECOND BOOK OF)
VESPA 1955-1968 GS & SS (BOOK OF)
VESPA 1963-1972 90, 125 & 150cc (THIRD BOOK OF)
VILLIERS ENGINE UP TO 1959 INC. 3 WHEELERS (BOOK OF)
VILLIERS ENGINE UP TO 1969 (BOOK OF)
VINCENT 1935-1955 (WORKSHOP MANUAL)
YAMAHA 1961-1967 YA5 & YA6 (WORKSHOP MANUAL & ILL PARTS LIST)
YAMAHA 1971-1972 JT1& JT2 (WORKSHOP MANUAL & ILL PARTS LIST)

VELOCEPRESS TECHNICAL BOOKS – MOTORCYCLE

1930'S BRITISH MOTORCYCLE CARBS & ELEC COMPONENTS (BOOK OF)
1930'S BRITISH MOTORCYCLE ENGINES (OVERHAUL & MAINTENANCE)
1930'S BRITISH MOTORCYCLE GEARBOXES & CLUTCHES (BOOK OF)
CATALOG OF BRITISH MOTORCYCLES (1951 MODELS)
CYCLEMOTOR (BOOK OF)
LUCAS ELECTRONICS BRITISH M/CYCLES REPAIR & PARTS (1950-1977)
MOTORCYCLE ENGINEERING (P.E. Irving)
MOTORCYCLE ROAD TESTS 1949-1953 (Motor Cycle Magazine UK)
SPEED AND HOW TO OBTAIN IT (Motor Cycle Magazine UK)
TUNING FOR SPEED (P.E. Irving)

VELOCEPRESS MANUALS - THREE WHEELER'S

BMW ISETTA FACTORY WORKSHOP MANUAL
BSA THREE WHEELER (BOOK OF)
VINTAGE MORGAN THREE WHEELER (BOOK OF)

VELOCEPRESS MANUALS – AUTOMOBILE BY MAKE

ALFA ROMEO GIULIA WORKSHOP MANUAL 1300 TO 2000cc 1962-1975
ALFA ROMEO GIULIA TECH MANUAL CARBURETED CARS FROM 1962
ALFA ROMEO GIULIA TECH MANUAL FUEL INJECTED CARS FROM 1969
ALFA ROMEO GIULIETTA & GIULIA 750 & 101 SERIES 1955-1965 WSM
AUSTIN-HEALEY SPRITE & MG MIDGET WORKSHOP MANUAL 1958-1971
BMW 600 LIMOUSINE FACTORY WORKSHOP MANUAL
BMW 600 LIMOUSINE OWNERS HAND BOOK & SERVICE MANUAL
BMW 2000 & 2002 1966-1976 WORKSHOP MANUAL
CORVAIR 1960-1969 WORKSHOP MANUAL
CORVETTE V8 1955-1962 WORKSHOP MANUAL
FIAT 500 FACTORY WORKSHOP MANUAL 1957-1973
FIAT 600, 600D & MULTIPLA FACTORY WORKSHOP MANUAL 1955-1969
JAGUAR E-TYPE 3.8 & 4.2 SERIES 1 & 2 WORKSHOP MANUAL
JAGUAR MK 7, 8, 9 & XK120, 140, 150 WORKSHOP MANUAL 1948-1961
METROPOLITAN FACTORY WORKSHOP MANUAL
MGA & MGB OWNERS HANDBOOK & WORKSHOP MANUAL
MG MIDGET TC, TD, TF & TF1500 WORKSHOP MANUAL
PORSCHE 356 1948-1965 WORKSHOP MANUAL
PORSCHE 911 2.0, 2.2, 2.4 LITRE 1964-1973 WORKSHOP MANUAL
PORSCHE 911 2.7, 3.0, 3.2 LITRE 1973-1989 WORKSHOP MANUAL
PORSCHE 912 WORKSHOP MANUAL
TRIUMPH TR2, TR3, TR4 1953-1965 WORKSHOP MANUAL
VOLKSWAGEN TRANSPORTER, TRUCKS & WAGONS 1950-1979 WSM
VOLVO 1944-1968 ALL MODELS WORKSHOP MANUAL

VELOCEPRESS TECHNICAL BOOKS - AUTOMOBILE

FERRARI 250/GT SERVICE AND MAINTENANCE
FERRARI GUIDE TO PERFORMANCE
FERRARI OWNER'S HANDBOOK
FERRARI TUNING TIPS & MAINTENANCE TECHNIQUES
HOW TO BUILD A FIBERGLASS CAR
HOW TO BUILD A RACING CAR
HOW TO RESTORE THE MODEL 'A' FORD
MASERATI OWNER'S HANDBOOK
OBERT'S FIAT GUIDE
PERFORMANCE TUNING THE SUNBEAM TIGER
SOUPING THE VOLKSWAGEN
SOLEX CARBURETORS (EMPHASIS ON UK & EU AUTOMOBILES)
SU CARBURETORS (EMPHASIS ON UK AUTOMOBILES)
WEBER CARBURETORS (EMPHASIS ON ALFA & FIAT)

VELOCEPRESS BOOKS & GUIDES - AUTOMOBILE

ABARTH BUYERS GUIDE
COMPLETE CATALOG OF JAPANESE MOTOR VEHICLES
FERRARI 308 SERIES BUYER'S AND OWNER'S GUIDE
FERRARI BERLINETTA LUSSO
FERRARI BROCHURES AND SALES LITERATURE 1946-1967
FERRARI BROCHURES AND SALES LITERATURE 1968-1989
FERRARI SERIAL NUMBERS PART I - ODD NUMBERS TO 21399
FERRARI SERIAL NUMBERS PART II - EVEN NUMBERS TO 1050
FERRARI SPYDER CALIFORNIA
HENRY'S FABULOUS MODEL "A" FORD
MASERATI BROCHURES AND SALES LITERATURE

VELOCEPRESS BOOKS – RACING

CARRERA PANAMERICANA - MEXICAN ROAD RACE (BOOK OF)
DIALED IN - THE JAN OPPERMAN STORY
IF HEMINGWAY HAD WRITTEN A RACING NOVEL
VEDA ORR'S NEW REVISED HOT ROD PICTORIAL

AUTOBOOKS WORKSHOP MANUALS & BROOKLANDS ROAD TEST PORTFOLIOS

FOR A COMPLETE LISTING OF THE AUTOBOOKS & BROOKLANDS TITLES THAT WE CURRENTLY HAVE AVAILABLE, PLEASE VISIT OUR WEBSITE.
www.VelocePress.com

Please check our website:

www.VelocePress.com

for a complete up-to-date list of available titles

www.ingramcontent.com/pod-product-compliance
Lightning Source LLC
Chambersburg PA
CBHW070558170426
43201CB00012B/1871